AF441222

SUCCESS AND MOTIVATION IN BANKING, FINANCE AND MANAGEMENT

BY

DR. CHARLES O. UKEMENAM

FCIB, M.Sc, Ph.D

FOREWORD

The book entitled, "Success and Motivation in Banking, Finance and Management," according to the author is another outstanding production – i.e., three in one motivational and self-development book. Like the previous books published under the series, it contains a large dose of entrepreneurship tips, ideas and knowledge which are germane for self-employment and job creation in our country and the entire world.

The book is divided into three sections, namely Section A, B and C respectively. The reason for adoption of this approach, according to the author, is to give adequate attention to the most important issues which motivate people into becoming successful and outstanding business persons. The author in <u>Section A</u> defines Success and Motivation, which are keys which motivate people into taking a plunge to venture into business and entrepreneurship. Other issues discussed in Section A, such as: Building Your Success Complex, Science of Personal Motivation, Secret of Personal Achievement, etc., are all very important issues which budding and even accomplished businessmen and women should internalize for their eternal welfare and prosperity.

Sections B and C respectively are full of skills and knowledge which both modern and budding entrepreneurs require currently in the areas of Banking/Finance and Management issues in the development of entrepreneurship and job creation.

In fact, I sincerely commend the author of the book for his painstaking research and hard work which has resulted in the production this masterpiece of a book.

I have therefore no hesitation in recommending this classical and inspiring book of our generation to all those interested in economic development and empowerment, skills acquisition, etc. Without any doubt, the book will be of immense benefit to students, teachers/scholars, administrators, businessmen and women, etc.

Prof. C. U. Onugu,
Department of Agriculture,
Nnamdi Azikiwe University,
Awka,
Anambra State.

<u>ACKNOWLEDGEMENTS</u>

Honestly, it is not easy to say a big "Thank You" to all those who encouraged or supported me in producing this magnificent book, which will awaken the entrepreneurial spirit of our people by changing their mindset. This book is another thank you to my late parents, who first inculcated in me the lasting value of education at an early age.

Their support and encouragement enabled me to appreciate education as a vital tool for wealth creation and national development.

My gratitude goes to Prof. Charles Onugu, my former colleague at the National Board for Community Banks (NBCB), Zonal Office, Enugu for his insightful suggestions/contributions during the production stage of this book. I also cherish the encouragement and support of Dr. JVC Iloh, my former colleague in the Department of Banking and Finance, the Institute of Management and Technology, IMT, Enugu. My gratitude also goes to my former colleagues at the National Open University of Nigeria (NOUN), Enugu Study Centre, notably Prof. Patrick E. Eya, presently at the National Headquarter in Abuja and others who encouraged me in the institution.

Finally, I wish to acknowledge all the authors whose work assisted me during the research I conducted, which led to the production of this book particularly: - Mr. Paul Meyer, President of Success Motivation Institute of USA (SMI); Mr. Robert T. Kiyosaki and Sharon L. Letcher, authors of Rich Dad and Poor Dad; the famous Motivational Author of the book, Think and Grow Rich, Dr. Napoleon Hill of blessed memory. There are also several authors whose ideas and work assisted me in producing this great book. However, I cannot find space to accommodate all of them as some are also mentioned under the reference page.

I wish to appreciate the proficiency and efficiency of Arc. Onyekachi I.Ejimofor who did a marvelous typesetting work of the book.

Indeed, I remain grateful to all of them and also to members of my family at home and abroad for their un-alloyed support always. I take sole responsibility for any errors and omissions in the book. Finally, I thank God Almighty for his grace and support. I thank you all.

Dr. Charles O. Ukemenam.

INTRODUCTION

This book entitled Success and Motivation in Banking, Finance and Management is a motivational and self-development book. It is designed to educate people of all classes on the "secrets" of achieving success and self-motivation in all their daily endeavors, no matter how small.

The author, through diligent research which spanned a period of over 30 (thirty years), coupled with his wide personal experience as a retired professional banker/Management Consultant discovered the urgent need for people to be properly groomed in the art of achieving lasting success in life. He also discovered that success does not just come to people accidentally, or through "good luck", but only through diligent planning, hard work and focus.

This is the main reason for the production of this highly educative and self-motivational book, comprising three sections.

For instance, <u>Section A</u> opens with a definition of Success and Motivation which is its main topic or focus. Thereafter, the book refers to success as a <u>journey of life</u> which is indeed endless, and shows one how to build your own <u>Success Complex</u> or Success Consciousness. The book then proceeds to discuss and dissect other important ingredients of lasting success such as: -

* The Science of Personal Motivation;
* Secret of Personal Achievement;
* Power of the Mastermind;
* Ten Commandments of Possibility Thinking;
* Power-Plus Motivation for All; i.e. – a very important ingredient for living a successful and worthy life.

All the other chapters in this section contain highly motivational and inspiring materials for success in all human endeavors.

The section closes with Pope Francis' contribution and ideas, titled: Happiness, Success and Opportunity. Another interesting contribution in this section is by Mr. George Orwell, a British writer whose real name is, Eric Arthur Blair. He wrote a sensational and popular book titled "Animal Farm", which was also referred to as, "all animals are equal, but some are more equal than others". This 18th century author also wrote: "Five great motives for writing books" (under chapter four).

I strongly believe that readers would like to know the reasons people still write books in this "Internet Age."

The three-fold purpose of the book are: -

* To promote reading culture amongst the youths, and Nigerians in general.

❖ Promotion of self-employment, poverty reduction and socio-economic development of Nigeria, through self-empowerment and entrepreneurship development programs.

❖ To promote critical and deep thinking habits amongst Nigerians, by using self development, motivational thoughts and ideas which abound in the book.

It is my earnest desire and sincere prayer that the book shall greatly enrich your knowledge and wealth, for our national and economic development.

Finally, take note that the cover of the book depicts a high-powered computer network, which like the human mind is capable of producing amazing results if properly programmed. This is the main thrust of the book.

Section B

The author, having been a practicing and professional banker of repute realized the importance of featuring some topical issues in Banking and Finance, to which this section is devoted. There is no doubting the fact that businesses and entrepreneurship, including trading (buying and selling) cannot thrive or survive without the banking and finance industry.

However, because of space constraints only a few important issues regarding the industry are presented in the book.

The section opens with a brief history of the origin of Nigerian banks, (pre and post independence era). It then touches on the Central Bank of Nigeria, its duties and functions, etc.

The book touches on Banker and Customer Relationship; it then poses the question: Who Is A Bank's Customer? The answers and more are properly highlighted in the book. Other important issues regarding Finance have been properly elucidated upon in our previous publications.

The book however presents other very interesting issues, such as: Mortgages, Bank Lending and Securities for bank borrowing. Financial Intelligence for All, and Why People Write Books. It is a must read!

Section C

Management Issues in Business

It could be observed that both Sections B and C are newly introduced into our educational curricular as a result of their inevitable importance in the world of business. As we all know, businesses can neither survive nor prosper without a proper management set-up, hence the importance of this section of the book.

The section starts with a Definition and Interpretation of Management, a concept which is widely known and used throughout the world. It also talks about the Scientific Management School; what other experts said on the topic and other related issues.

Topics such as: Bad Management in Enterprises; Basic Personnel Management and Office Organization are thoroughly discussed and dissected. The section closes with Organizational Structures of work organizations; typical organizational charts are also produced and discussed extensively. These charts which are also called "organograms," are very important managerial (or management) tools which enhance productivity and profitability in the organization.

I have no doubt about the abundance of knowledge (both theoretical and practical), which this unique book of our generation contains for your delight. You are also advised to refer to our Bibliography/Reference section for more detailed elucidation on the topics as may become necessary.

Happy reading.

Dr. Charles O. Ukemenam
(Author)

Table Of Contents

CHAPTER ONE

SUCCESS AND MOTIVATION DEFINED

INTRODUCTION

As we already know, Success means many things to a lot of people, depending on one's perspective about life. To aid our journey on this voyage of success, I consider it appropriate to firstly define this word which has a universal appeal and acceptability. Success is defined by the Oxford Advanced Learner's Dictionary of Current English Language (2002 Edition), as follows: -

The ability to achieve something that one has been trying to get or do;

To have a good result or effect that was intended in pursuit of a goal;

The act of achieving one's aim, goals, objectives or what was intended by someone.

It should be noted however, that various Dictionaries present different meanings of the word success, just as the word has varied meanings to every person. For instance, Dr. Napoleon Hill, one of the most renowned motivational writers of the 20th century, who after defining success talked extensively about "success-consciousness". Talking about success and happiness Dr. Hill stated that, "success-consciousness is the place where all achievement begins. It is a time in your life when you first realize that there is a happy and successful way to live". According to him, you suddenly discover that you can change or alter your life for the better. If you purposefully decide to change and then follow through your plans, you will attain your desires which lead one into developing "success consciousness" and more successes in other endeavors.

Now, having gained "success-conscious", you then begin to search for everything you could do, read or hear to satisfy that hunger to succeed in achieving that success or goal. In other words, it is quite safe to aver that success-consciousness is a trigger which releases the hunger or a serious desire for success in people.

As a matter of fact, I have personally read many books, spent many hours listening to tapes and records, I found a basic truth that methods and techniques change, but principles never do. It also applies to the principles of success.

FURTHER DEFINITION OF SUCCESS

Now, if you were asked to define success, what would be your answer? Perhaps you may never have thought about it. There are probably as many different definitions for success as there are people in the world. For example, if you were to ask a businessman his definition of success, he might say that being successful means making a lot of money, or making millions of Naira, Dollars or British Pounds/Euros.

A football coach may believe that winning the National League trophy in the year is the pinnacle of success for him. To a salesman, success to him means becoming the number one, (or best) salesman in the company for the year. A student's dream of success might be that golden moment when he/she receives the institution's degree or Diploma Certificate.

Success to the housewife could be her role in the proper up-bringing of her children and the successful completion of their studies, thus securing good jobs for them. To the architect or civil engineer, success would probably mean the design and erection of beautiful buildings on the city's skyline.

The factory worker may feel successful when he/she knows that he has given his employer a good eight hours of satisfactory work each day. To an aspiring young lawyer, a desire to become President of the Bar Association may be the ultimate success.

As we can see, success means many things to many people. Everyone may have a personal definition for success, but only few persons have actually thought deeply about what it entails. Success is obviously much more than any of the preceding definitions, because it involves a lot of planning (and action) for one to succeed. It must therefore be considered in greater depth and details to reveal the proper definition of true success.

It is equally important to realize that money earned through money-grabbing, 419 business, corrupt practices and illegal business transactions cannot be included in the definition of success. These are merely short-sighted view of "success", because having money by all means does not make a person successful. Recent events have shown that people who made their money through fraudulent and dubious means cannot escape the long arms of the law, no matter how long it takes. Imagine the level of disgrace and shame which the family and friends of fraudsters face when they are unmasked to the public. We should therefore not forget the good old saying that "honesty is the best policy". This maxim still remains valid till eternity, no matter what happens in the world. Fortunately, for us, modern research has shown that there are certain secrets of becoming successful through honest means and by following scientific and natural laws which shall be revealed in this book.

DEFINITION OF SUCCESS

Having done an introduction to success, it will thus be appropriate to define the word success. The Oxford Advanced Learner's Dictionary of Current English (Special Edition 2001), defines success as a **"noun"**. It defines it as follows: -

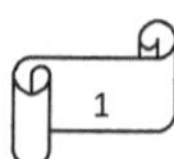

(i)   ...” The fact that you have achieved something”......

(ii)   The fact of becoming rich or famous, or getting a high social position”.

(iii) “A person (or thing) that has achieved a good result and been successful”.

The above-stated definitions are followed with some illustrative sentences such as:- (i)

    “I didn't have much success in finding a job”.

(ii)   “She was surprised by the book's success at the Book Fair”.

(iii) “She wasn't a success as a teacher”

(iv)   “The party was a huge success”

It is expected that with the above-stated definitions and illustrations, the meaning of the word “success” has become clear. Readers are kindly requested to consult other standard English Language. Dictionaries for further elucidation if necessary:

However, in spite of different and varying definitions of the word success, an anonymous writer, apart from his definition, concluded that ....” success is a journey .... an endless one from birth to death”. What is your opinion about it?

Dr. Paul J. Meyer, New York Times Best-selling Author added another dimension to the definition of success when he added that...” attitude is everything, if you want to succeed above and beyond”.

Continuing, he said that **attitude is a habit of thought** “who you are is a function of specific choices you have so far made in your life. Who you are is not determined by how you look, where you live, or who your parents were. You are where you are, and what you are because of the **dominating thoughts** that occupy your mind constantly. Having a positive mental attitude definitely propels one to succeed. You have the power to change, to be, and to achieve any goal you want, and succeed”.

MOTIVATION DEFINED

Motivation is a word derived from “motive”, which simply means – “a reason for doing something by someone”. People have different motives or reasons for doing whatever the person does. For instance, **profit-motive** is the reason lots of people embark on business undertaking, e.g., trading, manufacturing, marketing of goods and services etc. The main motives which make people embark on commercial activities is described as the “desire to make profit”, which can equally be described as motivation for embarking on business ventures, etc.

However, motivation is a general term which applies to the entire class of drives, desires, needs, wishes and similar forces which push or motivate people to embark upon ventures of any kind. Motives or motivators are forces or factors which induce individuals to act or perform, and these are forces that influence human behavior. Motives specifically refer to the drives, desires, needs, wishes, and similar forces that channel human behavior towards goals and objectives.

We can then look at motivation as involving a chain-reaction by starting out with personal needs, wants or achieving goals sought by the person involved. It is observed that without proper motivation people shall be unable to achieve success in their endeavors, no matter how hard they try. Experience has also revealed that people who wish to succeed in their various endeavors should possess a measure of self-motivation to achieve success.

It should be noted however that the word motivation is quite easy to understand and does not require a dictionary definition. Nevertheless, one may need to consult a standard dictionary if necessary.

The following are ways of attaining self-motivation which is very essential in achieving one's goals: -

(i) The individual himself should have the responsibility to motivate (or stimulate) his desire to achieve success.

(ii) Set a goal (or goals) to be achieved within a time-frame. Set short-term goal of say two to three year period. Medium term goal – four to five year period and long-term goal – six to ten year period. Please note that some people also make attainment of their goals a life-long ambition.

   For instance, Mr. Lee Iacocca, an American manager at Ford Motor Company USA had the goal of becoming Vice President of the company when he was 35 years of age. He pursued this goal conscientiously for 15 years before his goal materialized. Several people elsewhere have achieved similar feats through dedication and hard work over a period of time.

(iii) Supplement your long-term objectives with short-term goals and specific actions. For instance, your long-term goal or objectives should equally have short-term goals, which go on simultaneously to enable you achieve your main objective (as in (ii) above).

(iv) Learn a challenging new task each year. Learning to become a manager (or company Vice President) does not stop with having a Bachelor's or Master's Degree in Business Administration. A degree is the real beginning, not the end of learning.

Learning and applying the new computer technology and latest ICT applications will surely help you in achieving your long-term goal (as in (ii) above). For instance, a young Accounting graduate may equally enroll for professional Accounting course of ICAN, ACIB, etc.

(v) Make your job a different and interesting one by introducing some improvements and innovations into the job. With some imagination on the job, you will probably increase productivity and profitability for the company.

(vi) Develop an area of expertise on the job, you may want to be known as the best Accountant, or the best Engineer in your specific area of competence in the company. The company's management definitely will not fail to reward hardwork and dedication to service through promotions.

(vii) Setting verifiable goals for yourself provides you with a standard against which you can measure your performance in relation to your goals and objectives. Please, note that it is almost impossible to achieve your goals or objectives if you do not have a proper motivation, or desire to achieve it. This is the reason self-motivation has become a very important issue in looking at how to achieve success in life's endeavors.

MOTIVATION DEFINED

Motivation is a word derived from _motive_, (a noun) which is simply defined as follows: - a reason for doing something. For instance: one may say he had a _profit-motive_ in undertaking that bus transaction; or the man had an _ulterior motive_ in employing that lady.

Motivation is defined by Harold Koontz and Heinz in their book, "Management" 9th edition 1990, as follows: -

"Motivation is a general term applying to the entire class of drives, desires, needs, wishes, and similar forces. To say that managers (or employers) motivated their subordinates, is to say that they do those things which they hope will satisfy these drives and desired, and induce the subordinates to act in a desired manner." Human motives are based on needs, whether consciously or sub-consciously felt. Some are primary needs such as the physiological requirements for water, air, food, sleep and shelter, while others may be regarded as secondary needs, such as self-esteem, status or position, affection, accomplishment and self-assertion, etc.

Views of some experts on Motivation:

(i) Robert Louis Stevenson, a novelist and author of the popular secondary school novel/literature book entitled, "Treasure Island", was bedridden with

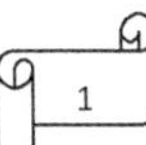

convulsion. But this disease did not block his **positive view of life**. On one occasion, he looked at the rays of sunshine hitting the walls of his bedroom and told his wife; "I do believe it is a wonderful day. I will never permit a row of medicine bottles to block my horizon (or vision). In all that happens, to me, I always try to see the positive side of life", he concluded.

(ii)   Also, never forget the priceless side of Rev Dr. Charles Swindoll, who stated that, "life is 10% of what happens to me and 90% of how I react to it". Truly, you cannot control whatever happens to you, but you can at least control your reaction to it. Don't see (or look) at what you had lost, but look at what is left in your possession and work with it.

(iii)   Walter Henley was a British Poet and Philosopher who wrote the prophetic lines, "I am the master of my fate, I am the captain of my soul". He should also have informed us that we are the masters of our fate and captains of our souls, which is indeed a reality.

And because we have the power to absolutely control our thoughts and actions, he should have also told us that our brains become "magnetized" with the **dominating thoughts** which we hold in our minds. Through this means, these "magnets" attract to us the forces, the people and the circumstances of life which harmonize with the nature of our **dominating thoughts.** He ought also to have told us that before we can accumulate riches in great abundance, we must **magnetize** our minds with **intense desire for riches.** We then become **"money-conscious"** until the desire for money drives us to create definite plans for acquiring it. Little by little, the truth has thus unfolded itself because until now it also appears certain that the principles described in this book hold the secret of mastery to our economic life.

(iv)   Late American President, Mr. Richard Nixon, said "a man is not finished when he is defeated. He is finished only when he quits; because winners never quit and quitters never win". This is an undeniable fact of life! A lot of successful people could surely testify to this.

(v)   Paul Meyer, a renowned American psychologist, motivational author and speaker, affirmed that... "90% of all those who fail, are not actually defeated. They simply quit!" Ah, what an irony! They quit before their time. So stay determined until you win, because you will surely win if you refuse to quit!

CHAPTER TWO
SUCCESS IS A JOURNEY

Introduction:

Success is simply a journey, not a destination! This theory was put forward by Mr. Glenn Bland, a renowned American Psychologist and Management Consultant.

He also described success as, "the progressive realization of predetermined, worthwhile goals, stabilized with balance and purified by belief. Success is a continuous journey – an endless one at that; the pursuit of success is endless, and it may even end at one's death". According to Mr. Bland, "success consists of three main things if you are to gain a true understanding, namely: -

(i) **Direction or Goal** – Setting your sights on the things that are worthwhile in life, and establishing a plan to continuously work towards their fulfillment and accomplishment.

(ii) **Balance** – Keeping the proper perspective about every area of your life; staying in harmony with nature's laws brings about happiness and success in our lives.

(iii) **Belief** – No man will become successful who does not possess belief in God and himself. The greater his belief – the greater, his degree of success. Successful men are believers"

With these three ingredients as our foundation stone, we have now established our own definition of success, (though there are other various definitions). This will enable us to communicate with complete understanding on this journey we are embarking upon. And when we refer to success, this is exactly what we mean. It is therefore quite important to commit these few words to memory. You will carry them as a guiding light, as long as you live and in this journey of success.

A famous motivational writer once described success as follows: -

Success is failure turned inside out.

The silver tint of clouds of doubt,

So, stick to the fight when you are hardest hit.

It's when things seem worst that you mustn't quit.

Success often rises out of the ashes of failure So,

persevere in order to succeed in life.

It is also quite important to state here that great and successful people lead balanced lives, which are made meaningful by belief (or faith) as already stated above. One of such personalities was Mr. William B. Walton, president of Holiday Inns Hotel Complex of the United States of America. On one occasion, while speaking at a State Convention of the Optimists International, Mr. Walton told the audience that... "You have **four great loves of your life**, namely: -

(i)   **Love of God:** - This love puts great substance and meaning into your life. This great love enables a person to live with himself. This is the greatest among the four great loves, and you must make a total commitment to this love if you desire success.

(ii)   **Love of family:** - **The** love of spouse, children and relatives is encompassed by this love. This must be a great love to avoid the problems faced by families in our modern society – (such as divorce, drug addiction, false living, etc).

(iii)   **Love of Country:** - You don't just inherit a wonderful country like ours (Nigeria). It is passed on from generation to generation, but each new generation must earn the right to keep it. You must develop a fervent love for your country (and state) if you are to be happy, and enjoy the fruits of its plentiful bounty. Your love for your country (and state or community) must be such a great love, a total commitment.

(iv)   **Love of Work:** - This must be one of your greatest love, for it provides the sustenance from which you live and grow. To obtain this love, you must engage in work that you properly enjoy, and is fulfilling to you. By making a total commitment to this great love, you can guarantee yourself, your share of prosperity and success", concluded Mr. Walton.

During his speech, he constantly stressed the importance of "attitude" as being "the golden key that must be placed in the lock of life".

The "Four Great Loves" are simply attituding about life. Mr. Walton's speech certainly exemplifies the thoughts of a man who knows the true definition of success.

Watch your Attitude to life

Mr. Walton above-stated constantly stressed that attitude is the golden key for success in life. Other development experts also harped on the importance of one's attitude to life, as an important ingredient for success. For instance, Mr. Thomas Jefferson, a Management Consultant in the United Kingdom, stated that... "nothing can stop the man (or woman) with the right mental attitude from achieving his goals; and nothing on earth can help the man with the wrong mental attitude to succeed". Don't miss Mr. Francisco Reigler who quipped that .... "happiness is an attitude, (a state of mind). We either make ourselves miserable or happy and strong – the amount of work is the same for all".

It is quite obvious now that your attitude in life determines your ALTITUDE in life; be positive about life. "It is your **disabled attitude** that determines your disability, and it is your disability that can or can't close opportunities for you" – says Mr. William Maphoto, a South African author.

Mr. Bland's Dynamic Success Plan

It is observed that very few people really understand what success means. Now that you do – put it to work in your life. Here are **seven dynamic rules** for personal achievement to help you put it to work immediately: -

(i)   **Let God Guide you** – Get yourself out of the way and let the great, universal creative mind of God give you direction. Have faith!

(ii)   **Establish a faith period** – Set aside thirty golden minutes each morning to engage in prayer, meditation and planning.

(iii)   **Crystallize your Goals** – Decide on specific goals that you want to achieve and keep them before you each day. Plan your day, weeks and months in advance!

(iv)   **Make a plan of Action** – Develop a blue-print for achieving your goals; set a target date for their accomplishment. Make periodic review of your plan.

(v)   **Develop a Burning Desire to Succeed** – Desire for the things you want in life will motivate you into taking positive action on your goal.

(vi)   **Believe in yourself** – you can accomplish anything if you believe you can do it. You have God-given talents and abilities – make use of them.

(vii)   **Never give up until you succeed** – Success cannot elude a will that stays in existence in spite of the pressures or adversities of life. Success comes only to persistent people, who do not waver in pursuit of their goal. You can equally make your goal a life–long ambition – it becomes a "do – or die affair".

Please, note that it may require completely changing your entire way of life, to apply the Dynamic Success Plan if you wish to succeed in life.

However, remember that successful people do the things which failures never get around to doing, hence they are successful in whatever they embark upon.

KEY POINTS TO COMMIT TO MEMORY

- You cannot achieve true success by deluding others (or yourself).

- Nature's laws are a greater force than the mere whims and caprices, (or wishes) of men.

- Truth will always be truth and it cannot be changed.

- True success avoids extremes of anything.

- Our creator has provided us with everything to enable us succeed.

- Great people lead balanced lives which are made meaningful by belief.

- Success is the progressive realization of predetermined, worthwhile goals, stabilized with balance and purified by belief!

CHAPTER THREE
BUILDING YOUR SUCCESS COMPLEX

Introduction:

Having agreed that success is an endless a journey which we have already embarked upon, the next stage is to plan the journey properly. In planning this journey, it is important to recall that every living being is endowed by our creator with the most intricate and baffling computer ever conceived. This is **your brain, or the mind**, as some people call it. You, and every other person own this unique computer, wholly and entirely alone. It can produce happiness and success for you in unbelievable proportions if used in appropriate manner. If, however the brain is used in destructive ways, it will equally produce disastrous consequences for that person.

This fantastic **data processing center (DPC)**, which you carry about with you all the time, was designed and created by God's infinite intelligence. It is capable of processing data stored in the world's memory bank, and contains all information – from the past, present and onto infinity (into eternity). This computer enables your mind to conceive any idea you will ever need, see the cover design of this book. It symbolizes a fast-paced computer, i.e., the human maid.

Dr. Napolen Hill, author of Think and Grow Rich, while discussing the unique attributes of the mind made this profound statement, "whatever the mind of man can conceive and believe, it can always achieve!"

However, despite the wealth-giving potential of the mind, most people use only about 10% of its potential. This is because, we occupy our minds with insignificant things instead of letting them to soar, as they were divinely designed, to do, - to accomplish big and important things. If you feed your mind-computer with negative information, the result will be negative and directed toward failure. But if positive information is fed into your mind-computer, the result becomes positive, hence computer programmers use a term called "gabbage –in, gabbage-out, "or GIGO. This means, we have to ensure that we feed our minds with only positive and worthwhile information if we expect good results.

In summary therefore, you are the sum total of your own thoughts. If you think in positive terms, you will achieve positive results; but if you think in negative terms, you will surely achieve negative results. It is noteworthy that wisemen and philosophers throughout the ages have disagreed over many things, but they unanimously agree on one point, namely: **"we become what we often think about"**. Ralph Waldo Emerson, a foremost American Philosopher, said, "a man is what he thinks about all day long".

Marcus Aurelius, a roman Emperor puts it this way; "a man's life is what his thoughts make of it". In the Holy Bible, we find the saying that: "As a man thinks in his heart, so is he".

William James, a philosopher stated as follows:

> "The greatest discovery of my generation is that human beings can alter their lives by altering their attitudes of mind".

THE SUCCESS COMPLEX

Now that we have established that thoughts have power, that thoughts become reality, and that by programming your mind with positive thoughts, you can become a positive minded person; it is time to build a <u>success complex</u> in your life, as follows: -

Step 1 – Success Doctrine (Wisdom)

2 – Success Oriented

3 – Inner Happiness

4 – Relaxed Mental Attitude

5 – Capacity to Love

6 – Mastery of the Details of Life

Step 1: Success Doctrine (Wisdom)

Success doctrine is a strong foundation upon which your future should be built. The Bible says: "wisdom gives – a long, good life – riches, honor, pleasure and peace", (Proverbs 3:16-17). "He who loves wisdom, loves his own best interest and will be a success," (Proverbs 19:8). You gain wisdom by becoming a student. As you read and study, you listen and do these things each day on a planned and organized basis. It must become a part of your life – you must eat, sleep and drink success doctrine because it is good for the soul.

Proverbs 9:11 states: "I, wisdom will make the hours of your day more profitable, and the years of your life more fruitful". Believe, and these promises are yours for the asking.

Step 2: Success Oriented

You will become <u>success oriented</u> when you have <u>success doctrine</u> foremost in your mind. You will understand yourself and because you do, you can then begin to understand others. Others will come to you because you possess a complete understanding of the natural laws of the universe, and you have the right answers. You will find that you "have a way" with people, and that you can make exciting things happen whenever and wherever you appear.

Your family life will improve, your business/working life will improve; likewise, your spiritual life will also improve. You will notice that you have become a wise person – one who possesses the wisdom of the ages, - a man or woman who **believes**, and is sought after because of what you have become.

Step 3: Inner Happiness

Everyone (or most people) in the world is searching for **inner happiness**. You shall find inner happiness as soon as you possess success doctrine and become success oriented. Because you completely understand the creator of the universe and his natural laws, your life will be in complete harmony with the world around you. This situation generates inner peace and happiness that will radiate forth like the glow of a candle light in the room on a dark night. Inner happiness and joy shall be yours along with other blessings which accompany it if you believe.

Step 4: Relaxed Mental Attitude

Once you have success doctrine in the frontal lobe of your mind and have become success oriented and possess inner happiness, you will automatically develop a relaxed mental attitude.

You will be able to cope with every situation, without frustration or anxiety. Virtually, nothing will "shake you up", because you already possess a relaxed mental attitude. Consequently, you will then have everything under control.

For instance, if you are a Sales or Marketing Executive, you will not become discouraged when your most important appointment becomes a failure. If you are a businessman or woman, you will not let the rigors of each day pull you apart; if you are a wife and mother, you will not "blow your top" because of home pressures (or stress) placed on you. If you are an athlete or footballer, you will "keep your cool" during the heat of competition while others are frantic and nervous. Yes, you will surely be able to master every situation, because you have become the possessor of a relaxed mind. The Bible says that: <u>"a relaxed attitude lengthens a man's life"</u>, (Proverbs 14:30).

Step 5: Capacity to Love

The next important step in the success complex is acquiring the capacity to love. Do not confuse this with the selfish humanistic love which prevails in our society today. If everyone had the capacity to love, based on the sure foundation of success doctrine, there would be no racial prejudice, no wars, no need for policemen, etc. Everyone would respect each other for what he and she is. According to the scriptures, love is very patient and kind, never jealous or envious, never boastful or proud; never haughty, selfish or rude. Love does not demand its own way, neither is it irritable or touchy. All the special gifts and powers from God will someday come to an end, but love goes on forever. These are the things that shall remain – faith, hope and love; the greatest of all these is love.

Step 6: Mastery of the Details of Life

The Pinnacle (or peak) of the success complex is occupied by the mastery of the details of life – a gift to all who possess the success complex. These days, most people find it difficult to meet up with their daily trials and tribulations. However only those who possess success doctrine know how to organize themselves through goals, plans and priorities to handle anything that comes up at any time. Those little things that bring stress and anger to most people are properly handled by those who possess success doctrine. He/she learns to accept what he can, and live with what he cannot accommodate, without destroying one's peace of mind. The man/woman who **believes** is master over all.

Please, note that the good things in life cannot be yours unless you pay the price to obtain them; - that price is success doctrine. **Believe** that you don't get something for nothing. Before going to the next chapter, you must accept the following principles: -

(i)   You are the product of your own mind and thoughts.

(ii)   You are capable of conceiving every idea you will ever need.

(iii)   You can change others simply by changing yourself.

(iv)   You can become success oriented and have inner happiness, display a relaxed mental attitude - possess the capacity to love and master the details of life by acquiring success doctrine (wisdom). Accepting these principles takes you another step closer to a life of happiness and prosperity.

The Power of an Open Mind

An open mind is a free mind. The person who closes his mind to new ideas, concepts, and experiences enslaves his own personality. Intolerance, the product of a closed mind, is a product of double-edged sword. It cuts off new opportunities and also lines of communication on its backswing.

When you open your mind, you give your imagination freedom to act for you; you also utilize your gift of vision. A closed mind is a sign of static personality; it lets progress pass you by and never takes advantage of the opportunities that progress offers.

Only if you have an open mind can you grasp the full impact of the first rule which leads man to any form of success: - **"Whatever the mind of man can conceive and believe, it can achieve it"**. The man blessed with **open mind** can perform miracles in business, industry and the professions, while the man with the **closed mind** is still shouting "impossible". An open mind requires faith in yourself, your fellow man, and the creator, who laid out a pattern of progress for man and his universe. The days of superstitions are gone, but the shadow of prejudice is as dark as ever, and only an open mind shall overcome prejudice.

Conclusion

You will no doubt observe that knowledge of Building your Success Complex is a **sinequa-non** for mastery of overall success in life. Mastery of steps one to six of the Success Complex is also of great importance in this our journey which commenced in the previous chapter. It is equally very important to commit to memory our key points to make this success journey a thrilling and exciting one.

CHAPTER FOUR

ATTITUDE IS EVERYTHING IN LIFE

Attitude is a habit of thought

Whenever the Olympic Games or some other sports competition takes place, we hear incredible tales of people who have changed by overcoming insurmountable odds such as gunshots, failures, birth defects, accidents, cancer, and more – to win first place.

How do they do it? What is their secret to getting up every time they are knocked down?

The answer is always the same: ***attitude!*** And not only do they have the right attitude, but that attitude is so ingrained in their heart, mind and soul that you will never shake it out of them. They have an I-will-not-be-denied attitude that will simply not be dispirited, discouraged, or destroyed.

According to Paul J. Meyer, the pioneer of self-improvement industry while speaking to some American University students on the topic: "Attitude and Motivation" during a seminar in 1992, stated that, "<u>the right attitude</u> is the most essential ingredient for success." Continuing, Mr. Meyer said that when he was just beginning his insurance career, he lacked both experience and a university degree. However, he was turned down by 56 insurance companies before he finally secured an insurance job. According to him, he had the right attitude, but unfortunately the company sacked him two weeks later, claiming that "he was too shy and too much of an introvert."

If only they knew!

Mr. Meyer went on to win every sales competition he ever entered and became the youngest insurance salesperson inducted into the Million Dollar Round Table of USA in 1991.

Many years later, to celebrate his 70th year, he climbed Mt. Elbert, the tallest of Colorado's 14 highest peaks and the second tallest mountain in the continental U.S. This might not seem like an impressive feat, but just three weeks earlier he had walked out of a hospital after having been admitted with a severe asthma attack.

Attitude Is Basic to Survival

Who you are is not determined by how you look, where you live, or who your parents were. Who you are is a function of specific choices that you have made. You are where you are and what you are because of the dominating thought habits that occupy your mind.

At another lecture in USA, Mr. Meyer told the audience that "Several years ago, a plastic surgeon friend of mine made a study of the people on whom he had performed cosmetic surgery. These individuals had come to him asking for some change because they were unhappy with how they looked.

As a surgeon, he gave them new noses, took away their wrinkles, or made some other significant changes in their appearance.

<table>
<tr><td>

"We can alter our lives by altering our attitudes of mind."

— William James

</td><td>

Life is 10 percent what happens to me, and 90 percent how I react to it.

</td></tr>
</table>

But he discovered something quite unexpected: Most of the people thought the surgery had been a failure because they were still dissatisfied with themselves."

The conclusion is obvious: We are what we think we are – not what we appear to be on the outside.

Attitude is Bone Deep

The renowned founder of Success Motivation Institute of USA gave another illustration during a lecture when he relived another life experience titled – "Lining the outside with the inside."

"I saw a movie once about a convicted thief who was offered a chance for a new life. After a complete makeover to change his appearance and to alter fingerprints, there was nothing left to tie him to his old self. He became extremely successful...for a while.

He reverted to a life of crime and was shot by a policeman. As he lay dying, he said, "The doctors didn't know, did they?

The doctors had changed him on the outside, but they had done nothing to change him on the inside *where all the significant and lasting change begins.*"

> You are where you are and what you are because of the dominating thoughts that occupy your mind.

Choose: The Positive or Negative

Each of us has an overall pattern of thinking that is generally either positive or negative. The pattern you choose has four profound effects on your life:

1. **Your attitude affects your belief in your potential for success.**

   A negative mental attitude causes you to doubt your ability to achieve, while belief in your potential makes you willing to take the action required for success.

2. **Your attitude determines what you think about when facing a challenge.**

A positive mental attitude lets you see a challenge as an opportunity, rather than a threat. It lets you see stepping stones rather than stumbling blocks.

3. Your attitude determines your confidence.

People with negative attitudes have so often thought, "I can't... or "I doubt...." that belief in their individual potential is non-existent. Each time you act from a positive attitude, your self-confidence is enhanced, your ability to achieve is proven, and you know you can succeed.

4. Your attitude affects how you see opportunity.

People who have a negative attitude have buried the ability to see opportunity. A positive attitude, by contrast, opens your eyes to so many opportunities that your challenge becomes which opportunity to choose first.

Three Components of forming Attitudes

The benefits of a positive mental attitude are available when you understand how an attitude is formed. Once you understand that, you then have the option to control the process and form the attitude you want.

Step 1 – INPUT:

Everything since birth is used by your subconscious mind as input from which attitudes are formed.

When you grow older and realize the need to change your attitudes, you obviously cannot start over at birth. What you can do, however, is to change the input. This has a way of positively affecting your mind and your entire body.

Step 2 – PROCESSING OF INPUT:

As you have heard what other people said to you and observed what they did in their own lives, you processed that information and chose your attitudes. As you acted on your chosen belief, it gradually became established as a habit of thought – an attitude.

My chosen belief is that I can do anything. I wake up each day without giving mental recognition to the possibility of defeat. This is my attitude and it affects everything I do, say, or think.

Step 3 – REINFORCEMENT:

When you make a tentative choice of an attitude, it eventually becomes firmly entrenched by reinforcement as you follow it day after day.

These three – INPUT, PROCESSING OF INPUT, and REINFORCEMENT – form a 1-2-3 series that naturally and automatically work together. There is nothing mystical about it. It simply happens.

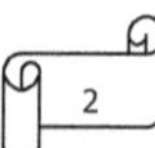

Can You Change Your Attitudes?

Suppose you become aware that some specific attitude is holding you back from the success and achievement you are capable of attaining.

Can you change that attitude?

Yes, you can!

Changing a habit of action or thought is not simple or necessarily quick, but it is certainly possible. ***You must first make a conscious choice to change!*** Breaking the old cycle of habit formation is the key to changing your attitudes.

> "Immense power is acquired by assuring yourself in your secret reveries that you were born to control affairs."
>
> – Andrew Carnegie

The following time-proven principle attributed to Samuel Smiles more than 100 years ago shows exactly how it works:

Sow a thought, reap an action,
Sow an action, reap a habit, sow
a habit, reap character, Sow
character, reap a destiny.

Where Change Begins

As you work to change your attitude, remember that attitudes operate on three planes: (i) thought, (ii) speech, and (iii) behavior or action.

Change can be initiated on any one of these three planes.

What you fill your mind with is eventually translated into the words you speak, and then your words are put into action. If you are not pleased with your results, you can intervene in the process of attitude formation at any one of the three points of thought, words, or behavior.

1. To change – YOUR THOUGHTS

If you want to change your attitude, change the way you think.

Changing the way, you think is not a new concept. It has been around for hundreds, even thousands of years.

To begin with, you must be aware of what goes on in your head before you can change it. Whenever you catch yourself thinking, "I can't" or "I'm afraid" or "That's too risky," stop and tell yourself, "Look again. I'll give this opportunity a chance. I can do it!"

Or make up your own success message, such as, "I know I can do this" or "I am a master at doing this." The important thing to do is to **break the automatic negative thought pattern.**

Attitude is a habit of thought.

Mr. Meyers, during another of his lectures told his audience that he once worked with a group of professional salespeople for six months, before he saw a noticeable change in their thought patterns. When their thinking finally changed, their sales increased.

2. To change – YOUR SPEECH PATTERNS

Listen to yourself as you talk. How often do you use negative words? How often do you express doubt, lack of confidence in your ability, or fear?

Write out some positive words to use the next time the chance arises. Be sure these words express the kind of success attitude you want to adopt. Practice long enough that you will remember the positive words when you need them.

3. To change – YOUR BEHAVIOUR

Everyone reacts differently to same stresses. A friend of mine was given a challenging project at work and instead of starting it, he went home and slouched in front of the television. When he realized what he was doing, he made the <u>conscious effort</u> to get started on the project, which needed to be done sooner or later anyway.

Intervening at the point of behavior is often the easiest point at which you can begin to make a change.

Where or when you intervene to modify your thoughts, speech, or behavior is up to you, because your personality is unique and your abilities are different.

<u>How to Intervene – Mind Power Principle</u>

One of the most effective ways to intervene is to make use of the Mind Power Principle to change your attitude. This approach uses a highly controlled practice of <u>visualization</u>, according to a specific plan, designed to accomplish a definite purpose.

Here is how the Mind Power Principle works:

A – Begin by spending some time in quiet relaxation. Put aside worries, fears and anxieties for the moment.

B – Read some passage you have found or one that you have written for yourself that describes the attitude or belief you want to adopt as your own.

C – Actively <u>visualize yourself</u> acting, speaking, or feeling in accordance with that attitude or belief.

D – Through visualization, you actually experience the behavior. You are eliminating   old,   negative conditioning and providing new, positive change.

Attitudes – because they are habits of thought – do not develop or form overnight. They develop over a long period of time.

You will not change them with one attempt. ***So be patient and give yourself time to absorb enough new, positive input to make the desired change.***

> "We are what we repeatedly do; excellence, then, is not an act, but a habit."
> *– Aristotle*

Plan positive reinforcement to reward yourself when you succeed. Positive affirmations serve this purpose well; here are a few:

That feels great! I can permanently change my thoughts, words, or behavior, about this.

I can see progress already. I am willing to persist to see even greater change!

My plan is working – I will succeed!

Measure your progress by comparing where you are now to where you were when you started. This comparison proves that growth is possible and encourages you to continue your efforts to grow and improve.

Then look ahead to where you would like to be as an added means of inspiration to keep growing, "stretching," and improving.

Benefits of a Positive Mental Attitude

Changing your attitude takes time and effort, but it is well worth whatever it costs you.

The benefits of a positive mental attitude are outstanding: –

☐ Increased enthusiasm ☐ Freedom from the limitations of fear ☐ Increased creativity ☐ Enjoyment in taking the initiative ☐ Maximized efficiency in utilizing your time and energy ☐ Boundless opportunities ❖ Abundance of positive friends and colleagues ❖ Exciting joy when using more of your God-given potential

Does having a positive mental attitude mean that you will never make a mistake?

No, not at all! But it is important to learn that there is more profit in making a few mistakes, than in avoiding them altogether. Those possessed by great fear of making mistakes will take no risks; and though they won't make any mistakes, neither will they learn or grow.

Positive Mental Attitude (PMA) enables you to: –

❖ Meet challenges head on, and you will gain even from your losses.

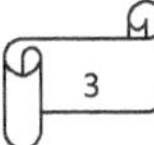

❖ Depending on your mental attitude, every obstacle, challenge, and problem has the potential to be the best thing that ever happened to you.

❖ Victory goes to those who dare to attack, not those who wait for opportunity to occur.

❖ And that is precisely why...*Attitude Is Everything in Life.*

WHY PEOPLE WRITE BOOKS

The answer to this question is provided by George Orwell, the English author of the popular book, "Animal Farm" – Alias "all animals are equal, but some are more equal than others." Mr. George Orwell said, "putting aside the need to earn a living", there are <u>four great motives</u> for writing a book: -

- The first reason is what he calls "sheer egoism", i.e., the desire to be talked about and to be remembered after death.

- The second is "aesthetic enthusiasm" – the desire to share an experience which one feels is valuable and ought not to be missed.

- The third reason is what he calls "historical impulse", i.e., to discover facts and store them for posterity.

- The fourth reason why people write books, according to Orwell, is for "political purpose" – i.e., the desire to push the world in a certain direction through writing a book or books.

Please note that the above stated reasons are <u>strong enough</u> to motivate anybody wishing to write books of any type in the world.

CHAPTER FIVE

SCIENCE OF PERSONAL MOTIVATION

Any person who wants to achieve permanent, sustaining success knows he must acquire and possess vast reserves of inner strength, determination and desire. He must have the ability to motivate himself. He must also develop personal motivation, because a man cannot hope to motivate others unless he is, himself, motivated.

Personal Motivation begins with developing personal courage, enthusiasm, **know-how**, confidence, and belief. Supported by positive attitudes towards his own abilities, the individual is motivated to create, to produce and to achieve. He sets an example of Personal Motivation that is the first step toward motivating others.

This chapter which outlines a simple but highly effective plan for developing and sustaining Personal Motivation, has been tested in the crucial and demanding world of practical experience. Personal Motivation has gained acceptance because it works! In this chapter you will find the nucleus of the principles that have made SMI the leading practical authority on both Personal Motivation and motivation generally in the world.

THE CLEAR MESSAGE:

Contained in this chapter is the crystallization of the SMI (Success Motivation Institute) – Concept; the foundation and starting point of the ideas and programs which projected SMI into the worldwide orbit.

That PAUL J. Meyer arrived at this conceptual crystallization at such an early age (in his early (thirties), is testimony to his genius in this field. The utter simplicity of "Personal Motivation" belies its fundamental power and the wisdom inherent in it. It should not, therefore, be underestimated, but prized highly for the insight it reveals of the secret of actively realizing the dream we all have of self-fulfillment.

To further aid us in the use of the Concept of "Personal Motivation", Mr. Meyer has capsuled it in the five-step "Million Dollar Personal Success Plan" found at the end of the chapter. There, in a one-schematum, we have readily available at all times the essence of this concept which holds the key to changing our life. It is a self-evident fact that some people seem to attract success, wealth, attainment, recognition and personal satisfaction apparently with very little effort. Others reach these goals with the greatest difficulty while still others never seem to reach them at all. What is the difference? It can't be physical and it is a proven fact that such ability isn't inherited.

Obviously, then the power, the capacity, the developed skill to achieve outstanding success must come from within the people themselves. It is the same quality that you possess to a greater or lesser degree right now, at this very moment. If you want to change your wishes into facts, your dreams into realities, your desires into solid achievement, the all- important answer is PERSONAL MOTIVATION.

Personal Motivation is exactly what these two words indicate; the ability to motivate yourself to accomplishment. Personal Motivation means the development of inner strength, conscious will power, overwhelming desires, and the determination to reach any goal you, personally want to achieve.

No matter who you are or what your age may be, if you want to achieve permanent sustaining success, the motivation that will drive you towards that goal must come from within you alone. It must be personal, deep-rooted and a part of your innermost thoughts. All other motivation, the excitement of a crowd, the stimulation of a pep-talk, the exhilaration of a passing circumstance is external and temporary. It will not last.

Personal Motivation is based on the scientific principle that each one of us is, in fact, the result of what we all think. The only practical world is that which is within ourselves, i.e., the world in which we develop personal courage, enthusiasm, skills, confidence, and belief in our own abilities. It is here that we sharpen our intelligence to motivate ourselves and to make our goals tangible realities.

Scientific research attests to the fact that the average adult man or woman makes use of only twenty-five to thirty percent of his total mental capacity. Consequently, seventy to seventy-five percent of the average person's brain remains idle and unproductive. Since all growth and progress comes from within, there is practically no limit to what a personally motivated man or woman can accomplish.

How do you motivate yourself? Where do you begin? First begin by a frank and honest self-appraisal at this very moment. Ask yourself these questions: -

Where do I stand now? Evaluate your strengths and your weaknesses, your assets – and liabilities. Put your answer down in black and white exactly where you stand now. Face yourself squarely, honestly and realistically. Do a SWAL analysis to objectively assess your present status or stage in life.

SWAL ANALYSIS: It involves an analysis of your: -

i.   Strengths? ii.
     Weaknesses;
iii. Assets And iv.
     Liabilities

- What are your strengths?
- What are your weaknesses? ☐ What are your assets and
  ☐ What are your liabilities?

1. CRYSTALLIZE YOUR THINKING – SET GOALS

Determine what specific goals you want to achieve; short-range, long-range, tangible goals and intangible goals. Then, write this information down in black and white. Writing crystallizes thought, and thought motivates action.

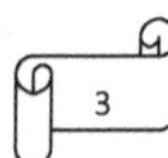

Be specific about your goals. Don't generalize or use vague terms. **Use vivid imagining and picturize**. We must develop the faculty of seeing with our mind's eye; seeing concisely exactly what we imagine: what we want. There is a universal law; that is, we tend to draw to ourselves that which we set out for ourselves. No man can attract to himself what his thought repels. We become precisely that which we imagine ourselves to be. Low aim is only low self-concept expressing itself.

When your goals are clear and vivid, they act as a magnet to draw you to them. Goal setting is the most important positive action of your life. When you have written your goals down, dedicate yourself to its attainment with honest zeal and singleness of purpose; with unswerving one – track Manship.

When you set definite goals, you're forming your own Personal Plan of Action that will put theory into practice, turn knowledge into know-how and thought into action. **A plan of Action discourages procrastination and creates within you an inspirational discontent. It will motivate you to greater utilization of your full potential. A plan of action, when you personalize it, enables you to sense the limitless power of your talents, abilities, and capacity to change. It provides the means for you to emerge from hindering circumstances that have heretofore stopped you, and to establish a personal success direction.**

2. **DEVELOP A PLAN OF ACTION, (OR ACTION PLAN) FOR ACHIEVING YOUR GOAL, AND A DEADLINE FOR ITS ATTAINMENT.**

This detailed plan is the road map, the design, the time template that will guide you to your goal. The plan must necessarily list the obstacles and roadblocks between where you are now and where you want to go, and also, how you intend to get around them, through them, or over them.

Be frank with yourself. Remember your strengths and your weaknesses, your assets and liabilities. Write them down, very clearly, your way around the obstacles and roadblocks.

Another important point in this part of the plan is pinpointing the talents and skills you now possess, and how you intend to improve them. Also needed are a specific schedule of time-organization, and how you intend to improve them. Put down every step and move, day by day, week by week, month by month. You will need them to check on the progress you are making from time-to-time.

Develop a positive attitude of "I will not be denied". Determination will not eliminate all of your problems but it will give you an attitude of stick-to-itiveness and perseverance. Thus you will create the success for which you are striving. With this kind of attitude, you will be thankful for problems because you can always turn them into procedures and proceed to the next step of your journey.

3. DEVELOP A SINCERE DESIRE FOR THE THINGS YOU WANT IN LIFE

A burning desire is the greatest motivator of every human action. Unquestionably, the degree of success you achieve depends on the amount of sincere desire you have. True desire will strengthen your resolve to attain your specified goals in all six areas of your life, and not just those in which it is easy to make progress.

Desire is akin to thirst. When you visualize exactly what you want in each area of your life, desire will add strength to your purpose. It will improve your self image. Also, at this point, you can determine the very real difference between "wish" and "desire". You can discover the difference easily by asking yourself these three questions:

a. What are the obstacles and roadblocks I will personally have to overcome to achieve my goals?

b. What are the rewards for me personally if I attain them?

c. Is it worth it to me?
   If your overall answer is "yes", you will know you have genuine desire.

4. DEVELOP SUPREME CONFIDENCE IN YOURSELF AND YOUR OWN ABILITIES

Confidence in yourself helps you to deal honestly with your shortcomings and compels you consistently to make corrections. **Confidence comes from experience. Experience comes from know-how and comes from having the courage to submit yourself to obstacles, situations, and circumstances where the average person shies away.**

People, who lack confidence, are not goal directed or oriented, and spend an entire lifetime standing on the sidelines as passive bystanders. Confidence stimulates your creative imagination. No matter what you undertake, you will never do it properly until you think you can. You will never master it until you have the confidence in yourself to do the deed first in your own mind. It must be mentally accomplished before it can be materially accomplished.

The primary element at the beginning of any enterprise, the one fact which will guarantee its success, is confidence in the beginning that it can be done.

The major difference between high achievement and failure is confidence – your self-image. This is what sells you and your ideas. It builds your success power. We either succeed at failure, or succeed at success. Both of these results are outward expressions of the attitude you hold toward them. You can either "think rich" or "think poor", abundance or lack, poverty or plenty, the choice is yours!

We are all creatures of habit. When we consistently maintain success-attitudes toward every situation and circumstances, we rapidly develop success habits. We make fewer mistakes. We make small mistakes. We make faster corrections and adjustments, because we have a success consciousness and a goal directed attitude.

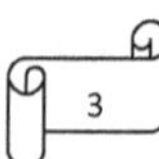

The degree of success which you attain is governed solely by the amount of habitual determination you expend. Every time you say to yourself, "I can do it and will do it", you are strengthening your determination. You are forming a habit of thinking which will manifest itself in action habits of success. You are constructing your determination and personally motivating yourself to success. You are forming the daily habit of sustained effort, controlled attention, and concentrated energy.

You can prove this very easily by observing any successful person you know. They succeed in everything they do because they never gave mental recognition to the possibility of failure.

5. **DEVELOP A DOGGED DETERMINATION TO FOLLOW THROUGH ON YOUR PLAN, REGARDLESS OF OBSTACLES, CRITICISMS OR CIRCUMSTANCES, OR WHAT OTHER PEOPLE SAY, THINK OR DO.**

Determination is persistency. If you make a decision, plan a course of action or make a resolution and then ignore your intention, you will form a habit of failure. When you make up your mind to follow your plan of personal motivation, do it. Let nothing or no-one interfere. Do whatever you personally have to do to get the job done.

In point number three, when you asked yourself the question, "Is it worth it to me"? and you answered, "Yes", there can now be no circumstances that can prevent you from reaching your goals. You can further develop your determination by reviewing your written plan often, by concentrating on the rewards. Thus, your desire and determination will stimulate a ceaseless flow of dynamic, powerful and positive direction to keep you on course until your aims are realized.

If you actually know your present strengths and weaknesses, if you definitely know what you want in each of the six areas of your life, know the short-range and long-range goals, the tangibles and intangibles, why is it that you do not have them now? Obviously, it is because there are some obstacles and roadblocks in your way. What are they? What is it that stands between you and the achievement of your goal? What are the ways around these roadblocks? What are you doing about it? It is easy to generalize and hope. That is little more than wishful thinking. The power of personal motivation comes through a definite personalized Plan of Action and the application of that plan every day of your life.

It is your **attitude of mind** that determines your reaction to everything you experience in life. If you develop a successful attitude towards everything you do and say, you will create the success for which you are striving. You will magnetize the condition you seek. **A person who is success-minded has a success consciousness and success-awareness. He lives with positive expectancy. He lives by the law of attraction. He magnetizes his condition.**

6. POSITIVE EXPECTANCY

When you apply these five points in a plan for your own personal motivation, when you develop success attitudes, success habits, and have a Plan of Action, you will find yourself living with **positive expectancy**.

There is an irresistible Law of Force that governs every human action. It is called the Law of Attraction and operates with mathematical certainty. We attract what we think. Every negative thought has a negative result. On the other hand, positive thoughts are the basis for success attitudes, and success habits which lead directly to positive expectancy in everything we do. Positive expectation, of course, must come from a sincere, honest, belief, a no limitations belief in yourself and your ability; a no limitations belief in everyone with whom you come in contact; a no limitations belief in conditions and circumstances. In other words, an attitude that refuses to accept limitation in any way, shape, form or manner.

With positive expectancy, you will wake up in the morning figuring out ways things can be done instead of ways they can't be done. You will look to your strength instead of your weakness; your power instead of your problems. You will enter each day without giving mental recognition to the possibility of defeat. You will see potentials and possibilities you couldn't see previously. You will withhold judgment. You will be a better listener. Your words, your tone and your actions will stop contradicting each other. You will be understood. You will stop being misunderstood. You will enter the arena of life with greater dignity, greater confidence and greater pride.

Your decision-making faculties will be clear. Your judgment will be both discerning and fair. There will be less margin for error and you will be sought after for advice. These are just a few of the many benefits you will receive with a Plan of Action based on personal motivation. This is what personal motivation means. The ability to live and work each day of your life in the brilliant sunshine of positive expectancy.

> *"Whatever you vividly imagine, ardently desire, sincerely believe,*
> *and enthusiastically act upon... must inevitably come to pass!"*

7. THE MILLION DOLLAR PERSONAL SUCCESS PLAN... 1. CRYSTALLIZE YOUR THINKING

...Determine what **specific goal or goals** you want to achieve. Then dedicate yourself to its attainment with unswerving singleness of purpose, the trenchant zeal of a crusader.

2. DEVELOP A PLAN FOR ACHIEVING YOUR GOAL, AND A DEADLINE FOR ITS ATTAINMENT.

Plan your progress carefully: hour-by-hour, day-by-day, month-by-month. Organized activity and maintained enthusiasm are the well-springs of your power.

3. DEVELOP SINCERE DESIRE FOR THE THINGS YOU WANT IN LIFE.

A burning desire is the greatest motivator of every human action. The desire for success implants "success-consciousness", which in turn, creates a vigorous and everincreasing "habit of success".

4. DEVELOP SUPREME CONFIDENCE IN YOUR-SELF AND YOUR OWN ABILITIES.

Enter every activity without giving mental recognition to the possibility of defeat. **Concentrate on your strengths, instead of your weakness... concentrate on your powers, instead of your problems.**

5. Develop a dogged determination to follow through on your plan, regardless of obstacles, criticism or circumstances or what other people say, think or do.

Construct your determination with sustained effort, controlled attention, and concentrated energy.

OPPORTUNITIES never come to those who wait... they are captured by those who dare to ATTACK.

Adapted with permission from "Personal
Motivation", By Mr. Paul J. Meyer, Founder of SMI,
USA.

CHAPTER SIX

THE SECRET OF PERSONAL ACHIEVEMENT

Introduction:

It is the opinion of the author that achievement, or lack of it, and the reasons behind each person's degree of success in life, are as different as the individuals who undertake the journey of life from birth to death.

Circumstances of birth such as parental background, race and origin; early or late influences, schools attended, individuals encountered, physical and geographical situation or location, etc.- all contribute to the difference in the underlying pattern leading to achievement or failure of the individual in life.

Fortunate is the person, whose life's experiences include the opportunity for encountering individuals or books that help the individual to focus his or her mind on certain basic truths about personal achievement in life. Only a few persons were perhaps fortunate enough to have developed themselves through the guidance of masters (or mentors), who shaped their early lives towards the right path of success. But this does not however rule out the fact that other less fortunate persons cannot equally achieve success through personal efforts and commitment.

When an individual realizes the simple but profound fact that **aiming towards a specific goal** is the best assurance of "hitting the bull's eye, then he is ready to move towards success in his/her life's endeavors." According to Dr. Napoleon Hill, the American author of the Secret of Personal Achievement, "any and every created individual possesses the ability, if they follow certain guidelines, or philosophy which he calls the "Seventeen Success Principles". According to Dr. Hill, practical and sincere application of these principles, whether singly or in various combinations, has provided the blueprint for success for countless men and women throughout the world. The Seventeen Success Principles are hereby presented as follows:

1. **Definiteness of Purpose:** This is the arrow aimed towards the goal. What is it that you want from life? What is your greatest goal in life? The moment you take hold of this question with your whole attention, you then begin to analyze yourself; your goals and aspirations. Also analyze your present state of affairs, and how to achieve the goal (or goals) you have set for yourself.

   Who are you, what are you, where are you NOW? Being thoroughly honest with yourself may be your first step toward success. What road are you traveling? What are the road signs you see as you take stock of your present position?

   It is well to write a list of the things you want from life – such as good health, personal relationships you wish to maintain, the amount of income you desire, the amount you wish to lay aside for old age security, the kind of home, the kind of automobile (or car), the benefits you wish for each member of your family, etc. These are the major purposes you must define for your future success.

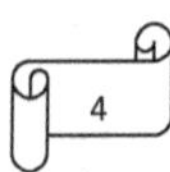

Map a one –year plan, five year plan, setting forth goals of achievement for personal improvement, self-discipline, sales goals per day, month, per year, etc.

Memorize these lists, going over them daily, early in the morning and just before going to sleep at night. Attempt at all times to remember that achievement of these goals will be determined to a large extent by your attitude and constancy of attention to them. Make your definite purposes a daily habit of prayers, conversation, and thought. By this you establish a **"success consciousness"** in your subconscious mind, and gradually your subconscious mind will aid you in carrying out the actions and reactions, which will lead to success.

2.   The Mastermind Power Principle

Having clearly defined your goals and purposes in thought and in writing, it is well to select an individual or individuals with whom you can share your plan for achievement. The mastermind principle is defined as **an alliance of two or more people, working together in a spirit of perfect harmony to accomplish a definite purpose.** The value of "gathering together of those of like minds" is self – evident. Harmony in a home results when a man and woman work toward the establishment of comfort and happiness for both.

Your mutual agreement with your employer to work towards high sales is a form of masterminding. If your major purpose in life is an ambitious one that extends beyond the accumulation of the ordinary requirements of subsistence, you will need the help of others in achieving it.

The Mastermind Principle is a means by which you may use the experience, the education, the talent, the influence and perhaps the finance of other people to aid you in carrying out your major purpose. Your mastermind alliance may begin with your association with one other person. The number of alliances you will require depends entirely on the nature and the extent of the purposes of your alliance. A "meeting of the minds" must be regular, must be mutually beneficial, and must always be harmonious in the basic matters of sincerity and trust.

3. Applied Faith

Deeply embedded in all the processes and the principles leading to achievement and success is the element of faith.

Faith is a prerequisite to progress of any kind. A man does not begin a journey across the room to get a drink of water without faith. Faith that his legs will carry him the distance required. Faith that when he turns the faucet, water will pour out. Faith that as he swallows, it will quench his thirst, **is it any less an act of faith to step out toward achievement?** The same Creator who gave us faith in our ability to walk to the water fountain can supply faith in our ability to reach goals in business and in personal life.

When the word "faith" is preceded by the word "applied", it means the faith one lives by and acts by – not something one believes in but does not practice, nor the faith in one's instinct to react properly to physical stimuli.

What is it that gives faith its powerful dimension? This is achieved when the individual seizes the truth that faith comes from the infinite God, the same source of power that keeps this world in an orderly continuous movement from day to night, season-to-season, tide-to-tide.

There is nothing, complicated about the method by which you may draw upon the power of faith for guidance in circumstances and goals you desire from life.

First of all, we must come face to face with our innermost self, honestly face the choice of goals, and evaluate the distance, the work, and the circumstances that stand between us and the attainment of these goals. The thoughtful man will realize then that many things must come to pass, a price must be paid, and help from many sources must be forthcoming, if he is to accomplish all he wants. Therefore, one must put the future, the intangibles, and the yet-to-be determined elements into the hands of the Creator - or else leave all this to luck or happenstance. The thoughtful man, the ambitions man, will then put faith to work, applying it to all those elements over which he can have no control as yet. This "letting go" of certain areas, yet with a belief that all will be well when the time for personality involvement arrives- this is faith. It makes for a relaxed state of mind, sound sleep, and a confidence that attracts positive reactions from every source.

Faith is the "Platformate" of human Endeavour.

4. A pleasant Personality – Positive Attitude Mental

Your personality reveals the kind of thinking you do, the ethics you observe, your mental and spiritual strengths and standards, the kind of life you lead. What constitute a pleasant personality? How may we develop a personality which attracts people to us?

There are many kinds of personalities, many kinds of attractiveness. Perhaps the most desired characteristic would be a positive mental attitude. "Smile and the world smiles with you, weep and you weep alone." Everyone has blue days, but the world will not long beat a path to the door of the chronically depressed man, the individual who always looks on the dark side of things. Look for the bright side of the street. Accentuate the positive.

It is been said that if you can make a man laugh, you can make him to like you. If he likes you, he will also listen to what you have to say in a serious vein.

Flexibility, that is being resilient to the constant changes and strains of life, without losing self-control is an art, and a worthwhile one. Sincerity is an absolute must. Lack of it is as evident as warts on the nose to the perceptive, sensitive, and intelligent observer. Promptness and decisiveness in decision taking usually denote clarity and directness of thought, self-confidence, and an uncluttered mind. Courtesy, tactfulness, tolerance, frankness, a sense of humor, a pleasant countenance, and a ready smile- all help to create and sustain confidence and good relationships; that is Positive Mental Attitude – PMA.

5. **Going the Extra Mile**

    This is based on the concept of giving more and better service than is expected or required, with the right mental attitude and with no expectation of immediate reward, or gain. The compensations are great, much greater than the investment.

    Going the extra mile ensures an increase in personal courage, self-reliance, personal initiative, and it builds greater enthusiasm. It is conducive to a more positive attitude and a happier, more secure position with one's co-workers and employers.

6. **Personal Initiative**

    Personal initiative is a trait much admired and if carried out with discretion and logic, can very quickly put you ahead of the crowd. Initiative, built on a definite understanding of what must be achieved, puts one in harmony with everyone around him, and with the universe as a whole. If one has a definite goal in mind, then opportunities for personal initiative are easy to find. Initiative is the first step – it is a self-reliant demonstration, which seldom goes unnoticed by those in authority. Personal initiative is self-confidence in action, and if you are moving toward a definite goal, it speeds your journey and soothes the way for good work to become easier and more rewarding.

7. **Self-Discipline**

    Self-discipline is training which corrects, molds, strengthens, and perfects. Your behavior and your attitudes are expressions of your thoughts. Much of our thinking seems to be uncontrolled, random thinking, or is on a semi-conscious level. From time-to-time we are aware of our "feelings". Feelings may indicate that we have been thinking strongly on certain subjects. When we feel, we become more alert because we have become aware of power, energy, stimulated by thought. We may be stimulated to love, faith, loyalty, or to fear, jealous, greed and anger. Self- discipline teaches us to direct the energy generated by our thoughts into feeling- and action- what will be advantageous and strengthening. Self-discipline will help direct our energy into the most useful, successful channels.

8. **Controlled Attention**

    Controlled attention is the act of focusing the mind on a given desire until ways and means for its realization have been worked out and successfully put into operation. Success comes after much concentration. Controlled attention to the power of our thoughts and to the energy we can generate through the mind is a vital tool.

    Prayer is not only worship: Prayer generates power, energy, unity, and strength. Thinking with another person on a certain subject brings new insights, new truths. Attention focused as one individual or several, brings power.

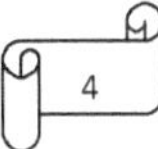

9. **Enthusiasm**

Enthusiasm is an emotion, the physical counterpart to our ideas. It begins and ends in our minds. Enthusiasm is harmony, and confidence. When you feel yourself taking hold of a definite idea, definite plans, then you become enthusiastic. Enthusiasm is a feeling of confidence, an awareness of a relationship between oneself and the source of power to achieve. Speak with enthusiasm and positiveness, move with confidence, and observe how enthusiasm grows and spreads to others.

10. **Imagination**

"The imagination is the workshop of the soul wherein are shaped all plans for individual achievement." Man's greatest gift is his thinking mind. It analyzes, compares, and chooses; it creates, visualizes, foresees, and generates ideas.

Imagination is your mind's exercise, its challenge, and its adventure. It is also described as the workshop of the mind.

11. **Learning from Adversity**

Adversity is a part of life. Every act, situation, or choice of our lives contain cause and effect. In adversities we have situations in which we are made very much aware of the effect. The cause may be known, or it may be elusive or incomprehensive. When we experience a very personal, significant reaction, a strong emotion is stirred within us, and we ask, **"why**"? **Every adversity carries within it the seed of an equivalent or even greater benefit. If we can capture this truth and accept the fact that this universe is governed by immutable laws, which are part of a creative force, no matter how difficult it may be to see the reason - then we can ride out any storm, which besets our lives.**

Your attitude in time of adversity determines much of its eternal effect on your life- for good or ill.

12. **Budgeting Time and Money**

Since your day has the same twenty-four hours in it as everyone else's in the world, you have the same opportunity as anyone for the skilled use of this time. Man has always had to harmonize with the world around him. But as the demands are made, the balance is there, if we seek it out.

There is less "time" now, because automation and faster transportation and communication seem to rush us. The art of budgeting time and money is one of the hardest to master, but most rewarding. The budgeting of money is a critical issue. Our eyes tend to be larger than our pocketbooks. How much time is there to learn to budget our money? All the time is available to us if we map it out.

13. **A Positive Mental Attitude – PMA**

Our mind is the only thing we can control. Either we control it, or we relinquish control, or we drift. We cannot NOT do anything. Being negative is doing

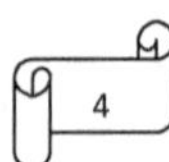

something. To govern your life, you must learn to govern your attitudes. How we react is determined by our habits of mind control and our attitudes. Are you looking for positive avenues to success? You shall find it, if you adopt a positive mental attitude (PMA).

14.   Accurate Thinking

Think about what you want to achieve. Determine how you will set about achieving it. Move towards that goal with definite, positive awareness and with faith. This is accurate thinking.

The accuracy of your thinking is affected by the hopes, fears, desires, and attitudes you allow to stimulate you. Organize your mind. Be aware of the power of your mind. Keep it controlled, and accurate, then you can be sure of success.

15.   Sound Physical Health

Your thoughts affect your health. Thoughts can make you sick, or thoughts can move you toward good health, good attitudes, sound sleep, and good eating habits. <u>Develop a consciousness of good health, and well-being</u>. Good thinking generates harmony within our bodies and generates physical manifestations of order and good system in our lives.

16.   Co-operation

Success within and without is an evidence of co-operation. All achievement is a form of significant and successful co-operation and teamwork between individuals. Co-operation is the beginning of all organized effort. Our bodies are healthy when there is organization and teamwork of all the organs. Our lives are happy when there is co-operation between us and the world around us.

17.   Cosmic "Habit force"

(The Mystic Element or the God Factor).

This is perhaps the hardest to define, but it is the principle that supplies the key to the understanding and utilization of all our inner resources. There are those who would call this the "**mystic element of life.** If you observe and believe that there is order in the universe, the rising and setting of the sun, the regularity of the tides, then you can see an example of a divine plan being carried out. There are laws by which the equilibrium of the whole universe is maintained. It is also called the God factor, that is getting to know the power of God in everything we do.

There are physical laws which make our patterns of natural daily behavior to operate in predictable order and regularity. Blending the natural laws of the universe with our own activities helps create that power, that force, that energy, which bring harmony, peace of mind, and success. You have the power to choose to take hold of the principles of success, or let it slip away from you.

Conclusion on the Secret of Personal Achievement

You have just studied an outline that can help you walk in the light of a new success beam to guide you to whatever station in life your hopes may demand. If it's a better-paying position that you need to make you happy, you may find the way to that position through mastery of the Secret of Personal Achievement. The author was an ardent student and practitioner of the Secret of Personal Achievement for many years.

If it is closer harmony and better understanding you need in your present position, the Secret of Personal Achievement can show you the way to attain it.

If the domestic relationship in your home needs improvement, this study can bring you and every member of your family the harmony, peace of mind, and understanding, which are so essential for your success in your occupation. The Secret of Personal Achievement philosophy will give you a better understanding of yourself and other people, so that you may be in a friendly spirit which inspires them to co-operate with you at all times.

If you have not been as successful in the past as you wished to be, this philosophy will help you to discover the reason and show you how to remove the cause or causes.

If you are in business for yourself, you can learn how to convert your customers into friendly workers, who will bring you other customers. If you are a teacher, the Secret of Personal Achievement can give you that "something extra", which will increase your earning power and help you promote yourself into wider fields of service in your profession.

COMMON SENSE IS NOT COMMON

Many years ago, I heard a profound statement which ignited in me the passion for the wisdom of God which says that; "the age of Methuselah has nothing to do with the Wisdom of Solomon."

After studying the lives of both Methuselah and Solomon in the Bible, it is imperative for us to make up our minds to pursue wisdom and live by it; and to affect generations, no matter our respective ages. Consequently, I want to share with you 18 (eighteen) Wisdom capsules from a book titled "Common sense is not Common" written by one Mr. Olumide Emmanuel, a Clergyman based in Lagos, Nigeria. If these wisdom capsules are implanted into your spirit and minds, they will enable you operate in uncommon sense, which produces uncommon success. They are as follows: -

(1) **One Thousand Good Intentions Are Not as Powerful as One Single Action:** Life does not produce results by intention, but by action. Take positive action in order to achieve results.

(2) **Never Worry About What You Cannot Change:**

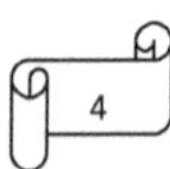

There are things we can change in life, and wisdom demands that we do something about them. However, one must also realize that there are certain things one cannot change, and to worry about them is a self-imposed affliction and enrollment for self frustration.

(3) **Never Insist on Doing Something which another person can help you Do:** Delegation of duties is the key to elevation, and division of labor makes it to end quickly. Insisting on doing what others can help you do, is not wisdom because it overloads your life. Try to delegate duties.

(4) **Never invest in something, which you do not understand:**
Wisdom demands that you get a clear understanding of what you are investing into, before you commit yourself or your money into it.

CHAPTER SEVEN

POWER OF THE MASTERMIND

As we earlier stated in this book under the title of "Secret of Personal Achievement," the mastermind principle was defined as **an alliance of two or more persons working together in a spirit of perfect harmony to accomplish a definite purpose**. The value of this **gathering together of like-minded people** becomes self-evident because it results in harmonious relationship which often results in greater achievement.

The master-mind principle is a means through which one may use his experience, education, talent, influence and perhaps the finances of other people to assist one in achieving his major goal. Your mastermind alliance may begin with your association with one other person, (or persons) as the case may be. The number of alliances you will require depends entirely on the nature and the extent of the purposes of the alliance.

However, a "meeting of the minds" must be regular, it must be mutually beneficial, and must be harmonious in the basic matter of sincerity and trust. This union leads to what we call the **Mastermind Alliance Principle.**

No man can accomplish enduring results of a far-reaching nature without the help and co-operation of others. When two or more persons ally themselves in any undertaking in a spirit of harmony and understanding, each person in the alliance multiples his own power of achievement. Nowhere is the principle more successfully practiced than in an industry or business establishment in which there is perfect team work between the board of directors, employer and employees. Wherever you find teamwork, you find prosperity and goodwill on both sides.

"Co-operation" is said to be the most important word in the English language. It plays a very important part in the affairs of the home, in the relationship of husband and wife, parents and children, and also in the state itself. So important is this Principle of Cooperation that no leader can become powerful, or last long who does not understand and apply it in his leadership. Lack of Co-operation has destroyed more business enterprises than have all other causes combined.

Examples of Successful Business Co-operation and Mastermind Alliance:

(1) Bill Gates and Paul Allen

Most people are perhaps aware of the legendary business relationship and co-operation which existed between Bill Gates and Paul Allen, his longtime friend. This relationship resulted in the development of computer software known as MS-DOS by Microsoft Corporation of USA in the 1980s/1990s. We are reliably informed that the business was so successful that Bill Gates, Paul Allen and others in the company became multimillionaires from this single product.

They then decided to split up the business. While Bill Gates continued to run his company, Microsoft Corporation, his friend Paul Allen and others started their own firms. Their former colleagues in the original company also became multi-millionaires while still in their twenties and thirties.

According to an article in the July 24, 2010 edition of Time Magazine, dozens of Microsoft millionaires set up Charitable Foundations in the 1990s. Bill gates then founded a foundation- Bill and Melinder Gates Foundation of USA at that time.

Even up till now, Bill Gates has remained one of the world's richest men for over a ten year period. He is a multi-billionaire who has devoted most of his wealth to humanitarian aid across the whole world, fighting poverty, ignorance and disease, and he is surely succeeding. The value of his company's stock has daily continued to gain ground in the American Stock exchange. Bill Gates' feat and success is as a result of perfect mastermind alliance and co-operation amongst him and his colleagues in Microsoft Corporation USA.

2. Dr. Napoleon Hill and Mr. W. Clement Stone

Dr. Napoleon Hill is the author of a highly successful motivational and self-development book titled, **Think and Grow Rich** which was first published in USA in 1937. Mr. W. Clement Stone, the publisher and editor of the inspirational magazine, **SUCCESS UNLIMITED** in USA, wrote; "more men and women have been motivated to achieve success because of reading Think and Grow Rich than by any other book ever written by a living author".

The publisher of the book, Think and Grow Rich also wrote in his book about W. Clement Stone under the following title, "He ran $100 into Millions". He stated that: "with only $100.00 (one hundred) dollars, the desire to succeed and by employing the principles in Think and Grow Rich, Mr. W. Clement Stone was able to build an organization that produces a gross annual income of over $36 (thirty six million) US dollars".

This assertion was made around the 1960s, when Napoleon Hill first became associated with Mr. Stone. In 1952, Mr. Stone's personal fortune was estimated (by Mr. Stone himself) at $3 million US Dollars. When the relationship ended ten years later Mr. Stone's fortune was estimated at $160 million Dollars –an increase of approximately $15 million per year for the ten years of their personal association. During those ten years, Mr. Stone's entire sales and, managerial staff was indoctrinated with the Science of Personal Achievement.

Many of the salesmen increased their earnings through the application of this success philosophy, as much as three and four hundred percent. Also, during the Napoleon Hill and W. Clement Stone association, they co-authored one highly motivational book entitled **Success Through A Positive Mental Attitude,** (Prentice-Hall Inc), which became a best seller from the first day, and remained so for a very long time. The book has been translated into many foreign languages and is still selling up till now in many parts of the world.

Note: Apart from the two examples of successful Mastermind Alliance Principle quoted above, there are several others which cannot be reproduced here for lack of space.

However, the import of the message is quite clear about the efficacy of this principle in the affairs of people in their business relationships. Everyone who handles this book should therefore realize the importance of Mastermind Alliance Principles, and endeavour to apply them judiciously in all their business relationships. Other important issues regarding the mastermind alliance principle are as follows: -

(i)   Minds Demonstrate Attraction-And Repulsion

It is a well-known fact to both the layman and men of scientific investigation, that some minds clash with each other the moment they meet one another. Between the two extremes of natural antagonism, and natural affinity growing out of the meeting or contacting of minds, there is also a wide-range of possibility for   varying reactions of minds with the mind.

Some minds are so naturally adapted to each other that "love at first sight" is the inevitable outcome of such contact. In some other cases however, minds are so antagonistic that violent mutual dislike shows itself at first meeting. These results occur without a word being spoken, and without the slightest sign of any of the usual causes of love and hate acting as a stimulus. While it is desirable, it is not essential to know the "cause" of this reaction of mind upon mind. That the reaction indeed takes place in every instance is a known fact, which gives us a starting point from which we may show what is meant by the term "Mastermind".

(ii)   Creation of the Mastermind Alliance

A mastermind may be created through the bringing together or blending of two or more minds in a spirit of perfect harmony. Out of this harmonious blending, the chemistry of the mind creates a third mind which may be appropriated and used by one, or all of the individual minds. This mastermind will remain available as long as the friendly, harmonious alliances between the individual minds exist. It will disintegrate, and all evidence of its existence disappears the moment the friendly alliance is broken.

The term "Mastermind" is abstract and has no counterpart in the field of known fact, expect to a small number of people who have made a careful study of the effect of one mind upon other minds.

The term first came to the attention of Dr. Napoleon Hill during an interview with Mr. Andrew Carnegie, the great steel magnate of the 1930s and 1940s. **Mr. Carnegie attributed the accumulation of his great fortune in the Steel Industry to the utilization of the mastermind principle. He explained that his mastermind alliance was made up of about twenty men.**

He said that they had given of their experience, education and their background for **one definite objective,** and that was the manufacturing and marketing of steel. This group held all the assembled knowledge of everything relating to the Steel Industry at that time. Mr. Carnage's primary job was to keep this alliance moving in a spirit of perfect harmony for the common objective. This narrative perfectly introduces the origin of the mastermind alliance principle as we   know it today.

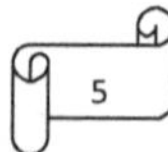

(iii)   **Espirit-de-Corps at work.**

From our definition of a "mastermind" we realize it is a mind which grows out of the blending and co-operation of two or more minds, in a spirit of **perfect harmony.** The word "harmony" is of utmost significance as it is used because two minds will not blend, nor can they be coordinated, unless the element of perfect harmony is present. This is the element that holds the secret of success or failure of practically all business and social partnerships everywhere.

Every sales manager, military commander, and leader perfectly understands the necessity of espirit-de-corps, a spirit of common understanding and co-operation for the attainment of a common goal. This "mass spirit of harmony", and of purpose is obtained through discipline, (voluntary or forced) of such a nature that the individual minds are blended into a mastermind. This occurs when the chemistries of the individual minds blend, and they function as one.

The methods through which this blending process takes place are as numerous as the individuals that are engaged in various forms of leadership position. Every leader has his own method of <u>coordinating the minds of his followers.</u> One may use force, another uses persuasion, and one may play upon the fear of penalties while another play upon rewards. The really great leaders of the world however have been provided with a <u>combination of mind chemistry</u> that is favorable as a nucleus of attraction for other minds, hence their levels of success in various endeavors.

Any leader who understands <u>this principle of mind chemistry</u> can temporally blend the minds of practically any group of people, so that it will represent a **mass mind,** but the composition will disintegrate almost the very moment the leader's presence is removed from the group. For instance, the most successful life insurance sales organizations and other sales forces meet once a week, or more often, for the purpose of merging the individual minds into a mastermind which will, for a limited number of days, serve as a stimulus to the individual minds. It is probably true that the leader of these groups may not perfectly understand what actually takes place in these meetings which are usually devoted to talks by the chairman and other members of the group. But meanwhile, the minds of the individuals are "contacting and re-charging" one another regarding the issues at hand through the mastermind principle.

(iv)   **Strength Comes from Unity**

It is a demonstrable fact that mind chemistry may be appropriately applied to everyday affairs of the economic and commercial world. Through the principle of mind chemistry, two or more minds may be blended in a spirit of perfect harmony and may develop sufficient power to enable the individuals to perform seemingly superhuman feats. **Power** is the force with which people achieve success in any undertaking. And also, power in unlimited quantities may be enjoyed by any group of persons, who possess the wisdom with which to submerge their own individual personalities and their own immediate individual interests in the union of their minds for the attainment of the desired goal.

When two or more people harmonize their individual minds to produce a mastermind, each person in the group becomes vested with the power to "contact and gather knowledge" from the subconscious minds of all the other members of the group. This power becomes immediately noticeable, having the effect of stimulating the mind to a higher rate of vibration.

And this takes the form of a more **vivid imagination**, and the consciousness of what appears to be a **sixth-sense (which is faith or ESP - extra-sensory-perception).**

It is through this "sixth-sense" that new ideas will flash into the mind. <u>**These ideas take on the nature and form of the subject dominating the mind of the individual.**</u> The minds of those participating in the mastermind become like "magnets", attracting ideas and thought stimuli of the most highly organized and practical nature from where no-one knows.

The process of **mind blending** may be likened to the act of connecting many electric batteries to a single transmission wire, thereby stepping-up the power passing over that line by the amount of energy which the batteries carry. This system applies to the blending of the individual minds into a mastermind alliance. Each mind stimulates the other minds in the group, until the universal energy becomes so great that it connects with, and penetrates the universal energy known as **ether;** which in turn touches every atom of matter in the universe. All the so-called geniuses probably gained their reputations because they formed alliances with other minds which enabled them to amplify their vibrations, until they were able to contact the vast temple of knowledge recorded and filed in the ether of the universe. All of the great geniuses, as far as the author is able to gather the facts, were highly motivated and psychic persons, though this tendency may not be too apparent to the public glare. Such experiments or enquiries will no doubt confirm the veracity or otherwise of the author's assertion about genius. Some geniuses are found amongst eccentric persons, i.e. people who behave extra-ordinarily.

The author nevertheless, believes that geniuses are people who possess **un-usual great intelligence,** and high levels of skill which "ordinary" people lack. Enquiries and researches into the mental make-up of geniuses shall no doubt be contributing a lot to the overall knowledge of the mastermind alliance principle in general and genius in particular.

Principles of Mind Chemistry:

According to Dr. Napoleon Hill and Mr. Harold Keown, Industrial Philosophers and Consultants based in USA, during their experiment on the principles of mind chemistry stated as follows: - "wherever you find an outstanding success in business, finance, industry, or any of the professions, you may be sure that behind the success is <u>**some individual who has applied the principle of mind chemistry to create a mastermind.**</u> This outstanding success may often appear to be the handwork of just one person, but on closer observation, other individuals whose minds have coordinated with his own may be found". Typical examples of this mastermind alliance are: -

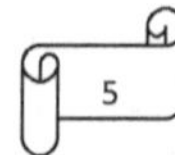

(i)   Mr. Bill Gates and his co-workers in Microsoft Corporation.

(ii)   Mr. Andrew Carnegie and his associates who pioneered large-scale steel production and marketing in the United States of America as stated earlier in this chapter.

Continuing, Dr. Napoleon Hill and Mr. Keown further stated that "power (manpower) is organized knowledge, expressed through intelligent action. No effort can be said to be organized unless the participating individuals fully co-ordinate their knowledge, experience, energy and expertise in a spirit of perfect harmony. Lack of such harmonious co-ordination of effort is the main cause of practically every business failure."

What were Henry Ford's Assets? The duo of Dr. Hill and Mr. Keown in collaboration with some students of a renowned university in America conducted a research and requested the students to write an essay on How and Why Henry Ford (of USA) became wealthy. Each student was required to make a research and describe what he believed to be the nature of Mr. Ford's real assets, and what these assets consisted of. Majority of the students gathered financial statements and other relevant information on Mr. Ford's wealth. One student out of the entire group of several hundred wrote: - "Henry Ford's assets consist of, in the main, two items: -

(a)   Working capital, cash, raw and finished materials.

(b)   The knowledge of well-trained organization, which understands how to apply this knowledge to the best advantage from Mr. Ford's view-point. It is impossible to estimate with anything approximating correctness, the actual dollars and cent's value of these two groups of assets, but it is my opinion that their relative values are:

(i)   Organized knowledge of the Ford Organization- 75%

(ii)   The value of cash and physical assets of every nature (including raw and finished materials)- 25%",

The authors, (Dr. Hill and Keown) were of the opinion that the above statements were not compiled by the young man whose name was signed to it, without the assistance of some very analytical and experienced mind or minds.

Unquestionably, Henry Ford's most valuable assets (like everyone's) were his own mind. Then next came the brains of his immediate circle of associates, for it was through the total co-operation of all these that the physical assets he controlled were accumulated.

Please note that Henry Ford was one of the early pioneers of motor cars in the world. He was born on 30th July 1863 in Dearborn Michigan USA. According to biographer, Mr. Charles Albert-Poisant, "the first things Henry remembered owning were odds and ends of metals which he always converted into tools. Ford's practical mechanical and engineering genius and his vision of machines replacing manual work had united man and animal under a single yoke for millenniums: it was already beginning to blossom. His dream was to take shape a few years later, when between 1895 and 1896, Ford drove his first car no fewer than 1000 miles; constantly submitting it to all sorts of tests to enhance its performance. He finally sold it for a mere $200 (two hundred dollars). Ford had no intention of stopping after his first successful achievement, but continued to go further and much further, until the present time.

Continuing, Dr. Hill and Mr. Keown asserted; - "if every plant the Ford Motor Corporation owned had been destroyed, including every piece of machinery, every dollar on deposit, Ford would still have been one of the most economically powerful men in America during his life time (and even beyond this period). The brains which built the Ford business empire could still have duplicated it again in short order; capital is always available in un-limited quantities to such brains as Ford's (and others also").

Within a short period of time, Ford had mastered three of the most stubborn enemies of mankind and transformed them into assets. These enemies of mankind are ignorance, illiteracy, poverty (and disease), especially in developing countries.

The source of all power is organized effort. Knowledge, when general in nature and un-organized, is not power. It is only potential power and the material out of which real power may be developed.

NO POWER WITHOUT ORGANIZATION

The astute businessman (whether literate or illiterate), not   only has recognized the importance of the <u>law of organized effort</u> but has made this law the basis of his power. Without knowledge of the principles of mind chemistry, many persons have accumulated great wealth by merely organizing the knowledge they possess. The majority of those who have discovered the principles of mind chemistry and developed that principle into a mastermind have stumbled upon this knowledge by accident; often failing to recognize the real nature of their discovery or understanding the source of its power. "Power" and "Success" are synonymous terms. One grows out of the other; therefore, any person, who has the knowledge and ability to develop them, may be successful in any undertaking that permits successful implementation or execution. The human brain and nervous system constitute a piece of very intricate system or machinery which very few men, if any, fully understand. When controlled and properly directed, this piece of machinery can be made to perform wonders of achievements; but if not controlled, it will perform wonders, fantastic and phantom-like in nature as   may be seen by observing the inmates of any mental institution.

HARMONY, THE ABSOLUTE "MUST"

Harmony is one of nature's laws and without it there could be no such thing as organized energy in life. Health of the body, as well as the mind, is literally built upon the principle of harmony. The life energy begins to disintegrate, and death approaches when the organs of the body stop working in harmony. **The moment harmony ceases at the source of organized energy, the units of that energy are thrown into a chaotic state of disorder and the power is rendered neutral or passive.**

This truth has been stated and re-stated, for unless one grasps this principle and learns to apply it, this chapter on the mastermind principle is useless. Success in life, no matter

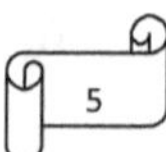

what one may call success –is largely a matter of adaption to environment in such a manner to produce harmony between the individual and his environment. If the reader feels that the author is putting him under stress on the importance of harmony, let him remember that **lack of harmony** is the first and often the last cause of failure, no matter the quality of leadership in the organization.

Every human being possesses at least two (or more) distinct personalities, and as many as six distinct powers may be discovered in one human being. One of man's most delicate tasks is that of harmonizing these forces so that they may be organized and directed towards the orderly attainment of a given objective or task: Without this element of harmony, no individual can become an <u>**accurate thinker.**</u>

LEADERSHIP

A leader cannot work effectively if there is lack of harmony in the organization, hence it is no wonder sometimes leaders find it difficult to organize groups of people to function without friction for the attainment of a given objective.

The leader who successfully develops and directs the energies of a <u>**mastermind group**</u> must possess tact, patience, persistence, self-confidence, intimate knowledge of mind chemistry, and the ability to adapt himself to quickly changing circumstances without showing the least sign of annoyance. **The successful leader must possess the ability to change the color of his mind, chameleon-like (if necessary), to fit every circumstance that arises in connection with the object of his leadership. Moreover, he must possess the ability to change from one mood to another without showing the slightest signs of anger, or lack of self-control.** The successful leader must understand the seventeen principles of the Secret of Personal Achievement and be able to put into practice any combination of these laws whenever occasion demands.

Without this ability, no leader can be powerful; and without power, no leader can long endure; because power grows out of organized knowledge. It grows out of it, through application and use.

A man may become a walking encyclopedia without possessing any power of value. This knowledge becomes power only to the extent that it is organized, classified, and put into tangible action. Some of the best educated men and women in the world   possess less general knowledge than some who are known as fools. The difference between the two being that educated persons put the knowledge they possess into use, while fools make no such application of theirs.

The true meaning of Education

An educated person could be defined as someone who knows how to acquire everything he needs in the attainment of his main purpose in life, without violating the rights of his fellowmen. The successful lawyer is not necessarily the one who best memorizes all the principles of law. On the contrary, the successful lawyer is the one who knows where to

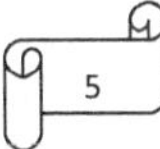

find a principle of law, plus a variety of legal opinions supporting that principle which fits the immediate need of a given   case. In other   words, the successful lawyer knows where to find the law he wants when he needs it. This principle also applies with equal force to the affairs of industry, business and other human economic activities.

Henry Ford and most wealthy men that we know, had very   little elementary schooling, yet were highly educated men. This is because they acquired that ability to combine natural and economic laws, and the minds of men to achieve power to get anything of a material nature they wanted.

During the First World War, Mr. Henry Ford filed a suit against the Chicago Tribune Newspaper, charging it with libelous publication of statements concerning him. One of the statements was that Mr. Ford was an "ignoramus, an ignorant pacifist" and so on. When the suit came to trial, the lawyers for the newspaper undertook to prove that their statements were true, that he was ignorant. With this objective in mind, they cross examined him on many subjects. One of the questions the newspaper's lawyers asked Ford was, "how many soldiers did the British send to subdue the rebellion in the colonies in 1776? **With a smile on his face, Mr. Ford nonchalantly replied: 'I do not know just how many, but I heard that it was a lot more than ever went back from battle".**

Of course, this reply brought loud laugher from the jury, court room spectators, and even from the frustrated lawyers who had asked the question. This   line of interrogation was continued for an hour or more, on various issues with Ford remaining perfectly calm.

But at a stage, Mr. Ford pointed his finger at the questioning lawyer and replied... "if I should answer the foolish question you have just asked, or any of the others you have been asking, let me remind you that in my office I have lots of officers who could give me the correct answer to all the questions you have asked, or any that you have not the intelligence either to ask or answer, by merely pressing a row of electric push buttons. Now, will you tell me why I should bother about filling my head with a lot of useless details in order to answer any foolish question that anyone may ask when I have able men about me who can supply me with all the facts when I call for them?"

There was silence in the court room as everyone looked at Mr. Ford with great amazement and wonder. Henry Ford's answer proved to all who had intelligence to accept the proof that true education means mind development, not merely the gathering and classifying of knowledge.

Mr. Henry Ford could not have gone into his chemical Laboratory to conduct all the necessary tests and analysis for industrial use, but he knew how to surround himself with chemists who could do this for him. The man who can intelligently use the knowledge possessed by another person, is as much, or more, an educated man as the person who merely has the knowledge but does not know what to do with it. With Mr. Ford's answer and address above-stated, the judges awarded him costs against the newspaper.

How to Form the Mastermind Alliance

The mastermind consists of an alliance of two or more minds working in perfect harmony for the attainment of a definite objective. To form a mastermind group, you have to think about the qualities of a good employee or friend. The following are some of the qualities required: - dependability, loyalty, ability, positive mental attitude, going the extra mile, and applied faith. The following qualities are also required in forming the mastermind alliance: -

Be sure that you are in complete harmony with the number two man, and the two of you agree on the number three man, and so on. This is very important, because you must take all the members into complete confidence. Each member should accept each other at "face value" and without any reservation.

(i)   Choose and **eliminate** if necessary until you have the right group working   in perfect harmony.

(ii)   Be sure you **set up a motive strong enough to assure getting the job done**. If you make a profit, be willing to share it with those who helped you in proportion to their contribution. Be sure that you go the extra mile in your dealings with the group.

(iii)   Ensure that you have a definite time and place for regular meetings to discuss plans and action to be taken. Any neglect here spells failure for the group.

(iv)   Keep perfect harmony; this is your job as a leader of the group. It will help here to remember Carnegie's major purpose, which was "to build men". Ensure that you create your own major purpose or motto, also.

(v)   Get into good terms with yourself. Do some masterminding with your "other self". It   recognizes no such thing as **failure or defeat**. This is an alliance you cannot do without. When you use the mastermind principle to avail yourself of the minds of other people, be sure that you must begin by taking complete charge or control of your   own mind. Do not try to be a lone-ranger or someone who prefers to work alone.

In conclusion, I wish to summarize mastering your own mind power, and the power of the mastermind by repeating a phrase which illustrates the sources from which the mastermind derives its potential for power. -

"Whatever the mind of man can conceive and believe, it can always achieve it. "the mind of man stated here consist of the sum total of knowledge which has been recognized, organized, and recorded by man since the dawn of civilization. It is available to all who have the   desire and intelligence to appropriate and use it. It is equally available to all who have taken possession of their own minds, and who seek success through the mastermind power principle.

Culled from: Succeed and Grow Rich Through Persuasion, by Dr. Napoleon Hill and E. Harold Keown, Faweeth Publication   Inc. USA.

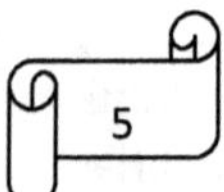
5

CHAPTER EIGHT

TEN COMMANDMENTS OF POSSIBILITY THINKING

Introduction:

What do we mean by possibility thinking? In essence, it is the management of ideas. It is observed that some people have never learned how to manage time, money, manage people nor themselves.

Possibility thinking focuses not only on the management of time, money, energy, or persons but on the management of ideas. Wise men and philosophers tell us that ideas are more valuable than money, (or physical cash).

What do we mean by ideas? An idea is defined as a plan, thought or suggestion, especially about what to do in a particular situation or scenario. It is further defined as, "a picture or an impression in a person's mind concerning a plan, job, or project," according to Oxford Dictionary. Psychologists tell us that about ten thousand ideas daily flow through the average mind, but a vast majority of those ideas are negative. **Possibility thinking therefore is, the disciplined separation of negative thoughts from positive thoughts by this criterion- that positive thoughts are those that hold undeveloped potential for something good. It is better to concentrate more on those positive thoughts than the negative ones.** The possibility thinker looks at every idea to see if it has **possibilities for something positive inside it.** This is the stuff of which millionaires and billionaires are made.

Conversely impossibility thinkers are people who instinctively react negatively to a possibility – laden idea. They impulsively look for reasons why it can't be done – they quickly abort an idea and forget about it.

An impossibility thinker is ready to give a thousand reasons why a project will fail, but may be unable to give five reasons why the project can succeed.

The point is this: never under-estimate the value of an idea, because every positive idea has within it the potential for success if managed properly. How can we manage ideas so effectively that we can be assured of success? It is only through the Ten Commandments of Possibility Thinking which follow: -

(1) **Never reject a possibility because you see something wrong with it.**
There is always something wrong with every good idea. One renowned Pastor once said that, "anytime God gives you an idea, you can find some negative aspects to it. It is amazing how people sit in a meeting and respond to an opportunity only by finding fault with it."

Don't throw away (or reject) an idea or suggestion simply because you have problem with it. Indeed, isolate the negative from the possibility, neutralize the negative. Exploit the possibility and sublimate the negative. Don't ever let negatives kill the positive potential that is within an opportunity. Nothing is impossible if you hold on to the idea that it might become possible some-how, some way, and with someone's help. Rev. Dr. Robert Schuler the renowned American Evangelist and Consultant said, "it is better to do something imperfectly than to do nothing flawlessly".

2.   **Never reject a possibility because you won't get the credit.**

Do not reject an idea with possibility to succeed simply because you will not get the credit. Decisions must never be made out of selfish motives or based on ego needs. They must be based on human needs and market pressures that transcend your own desires – and wishes.

3.   **Never reject an idea because it looks impossible**
Almost every big or great idea seems impossible when it is first born. The greatest ideas today such as motor vehicles, airplanes, computers, GSM, etc., seemed impossible at first. Possibility- thinkers take great care to nourish ideas and turn impossibilities into possibilities.

It is important to consider whether the idea is a good one; would it be beneficial for our country, humanity and the world at large? If so, then develop a way to make it beneficial to the world, instead of keeping it to oneself. Just because something seems impossible today, does not mean it will be impossible tomorrow. Could you ever imagine the present day wonders brought to humanity through ICT, Airplane, Internet Network, Digital revolution, etc.? It is because those ideas were not rejected initially.

4.   **Never reject a possibility because your mind is already made up:**

Possibility thinkers are people who keep an open mind and look at ideas as they unfold; - they are not involved in locked -in- thinking. People sometimes say... "do not confuse me with the facts, my mind is already made up".

This is rather an unfortunate statement because people who don't change their minds are either "perfect" or plain stubborn. It is better to change plans while still in the sea-port, than to set sail and sink at sea after leaving the harbor.

5.   **Never reject an idea because it is illegal.**

Some good ideas are impossible because they are illegal today, but do not reject an idea because it is illegal. You should also never violate the law. However, someone (or legislators) could even lead a crusade to change a law which has become obsolete. A lot of laws in the statute books today need to be changed because they are outdated. Legislators are constantly changing obsolete laws.

6.   **Never reject an idea because you don't have the money, manpower or muscle.**

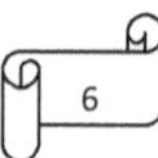

"All it takes to accomplish the impossible is mind-power, manpower, money-power and muscle–power", said an accomplished management consultant. Do not reject an idea just because you don't have the necessary power to actualize it.

Most successful persons have very limited resources, except the capacity to take an idea and bring together stronger and smarter people around him to successfully work it out successfully. It is often said that good ideas will attract the means for its execution, though with the right connections.

7. **Never reject an idea because it will create conflict**

I have observed that it is not possible to do something big and successful without creating conflict. One can never establish a goal without generating a new set of tensions which sometimes also create a conflict of interests or ideas.

Every idea worth anything is bound to be rejected by people who do not go along with the idea. To reject an idea because it may generate conflict, is to "surrender leadership" to friends or foes.

8. **Never reject an idea because it is not your way of doing things.**

For anybody planning to succeed, it is important to learn how to accommodate; to compromise; plan to adjust and change "tradition" because, these are all opportunities to grow. Learn to be equilibristic, maintain a balance between the limitations of the available resources at the moment. It is important to re-adjust one's budget; compromise your taste and review your life-style if you wish to succeed in your goal.

9. **Never reject an idea because it might fail**

Every idea worth anything has potential for failure within it; - because there is always a risk in everything. However, I have learnt from experience that with possibility thinking, success is assured if you do what you are expected to do.

Experience has also made me appreciate the fact that success is never certain; failure is not final, and no condition is permanent. **"Success is not carved in granite (or precious stones), it is always molded in clay" according to Rev. Dr. Robert H. Schuller of USA. "You should never reject an idea because there is some risk involved in it. You isolate the risk, insulate it, and eventually eliminate it", concluded Rev. Dr. R. H. Schuller the Great Self-Motivation expert.**

10 **Never reject an idea because it is sure to succeed.**

There are people today who reject an idea, (or an opportunity of occupying a very important position), because they do not want to enjoy the limelight and fame which it would bring to him/her. They simply, reject the idea on the ground of being humble, and afraid of withstanding the attendant popularly, glory and honor that goes with success.

Some people may describe high office and material success as "vanity" or being materialistic. This is not a healthy approach to life, no matter how one looks at it. To

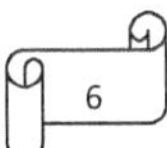

choose poverty instead of prosperity, failure instead of success, low achievement instead of top-of-the ladder achievement, simply for the sake of being humble, is unchristian. It is totally dumb, because only successful people can help people who are failing and require help. Only winners will survive to give food to the hungry.

Conclusion:

The Ten Commandments for possibility thinking are akin to what the Holy Bible contains, where it says... "If you have faith as a mustard seed, you will say to this mountain, "Move from here to there, and it will move; and nothing will be impossible for you." (Matt. 17:20).

Possibility Thinking Poem:

When faced with a mountain, I will not quit!
I will keep on striving until I climb over,
Find a pass through and tunnel underneath –
Or simply stay and turn the mountain into a gold mine, With
God's help, of course, I will succeed.

On Your Future

The easiest or cheapest way up is to forget the past, Make
the best of today and be excited about tomorrow.
Anytime you hide in worry, your future becomes uncertain.

CHAPTER NINE

POWER-PLUS MOTIVATION FOR ALL

This collection of short verses has been called by different names, viz: - success vitamins, distilled wisdom, epigrams, proverbs, etc. Regardless of the name you choose, you will definitely be able to increase your power for success by the means of <u>auto-suggestion; i.e. – by constantly repeating some of these statements regularly to yourself until they become a part of you</u>. The statements have to become **internalized** in your mind through applying the system called PMA (Positive Mental Attitude) in order to become effective. Some of these statements have been gleaned from the Napoleon Hill Golden Rule Magazine, the Science of Personal Achievement, the memory bank of our mind and experience of the author.

The collections are prepared with the hope that each person who reads them will be fully enriched in body, mind, and spirit; for as the great philosopher Socrates has said, "wisdom adorns riches and softens poverty". These proverbs are **mind conditioners**; read them very thoughtfully and make them your own. Then observe how other people definitely and quickly give you their friendly co-operation. We wish you abundance of courage, peace and faith. If you have these states of mind, all other things that you need will naturally come to you when you need them. These collections of success vitamins are arranged in alphabetical order for your delight. Read on!

Accurate Thinking

How can you judge others accurately if you have not learned to judge yourself accurately, through accurate thinking? The person who thinks before he acts seldom has to apologize for his actions. Thinking your way through your problems is safer than wishing your way through. The person who thinks the whole world is wrong might be surprised at what the world thinks of him. Many men who think they have arrived are surprised to learn that they have been traveling in reverse gear. You may as well not listen if you don't think before you act but be careful not to tangle with the man who thinks before he acts. Trying to convince the man who doesn't think, its love's labor lost.

Optimism is a magnet. If you stay positive, good things and good people will be drawn (or attracted) to you. – Mary Lou Retton

Action

Watch the man ahead of you, and you will learn why he is ahead. Then emulate him. The man who does not reach decisions promptly when he has all the necessary facts in hand, cannot be depended on to carry out decisions after he makes them.

If you wish a job to be done properly and well, get a busy man to do it. The idle man knows too many substitutes and shortcuts. The man who only does enough work to "get by", seldom gets much than he puts into the job. Good intentions are useless until they are expressed in appropriate action. It takes more than a name on a church membership to make one a Christian.

6

Believing

You can do it if you believe you can. If you don't believe it yourself, don't ask anybody else to do so. A man comes finally to believe anything he tells himself often enough, even if it is not true, might throws itself on the side of those who believe in what is right.

Cautiousness

Be cautions of the man from whom dogs and children shrink with fear. Over-caution is bad as no caution at all. It makes other people suspicious of such a person. Look carefully to see if the pasture on the other side of the fence appears greener, for there may be thorns mixed with the grass. Look the other fellow carefully who is trying to sell you his way of life, to make sure his way is as good as yours.

Challenge

Render more and better service than is expected of you if you wish to attract quick and permanent promotion, or customers. Every time you perform a task, try to excel your last performance, and very soon you will excel above those around you. Who told you it could not be done, and what great achievements has he performed that qualified him to set up limitations for you? Never tear down anything unless you are prepared to build something better in its place.

In the hour of defeat, many men have discovered their true greatness by accepting defeat (or failure), only as a challenge to try again.

Your Chief Aim or Goal

What do you want from life, and what have you to give in return that entitles you to it? The successful man keeps his mind fixed on what he wants in life-not what he does not want. One lady called Peggy Joyce in USA married four millionaires, one after another, because she knew what she wanted and refused to accept substitutes. The only permanent thing in the entire universe is what a man (or woman) sets up in his own mind.

Never mind what you have done in the past. What matters now is what you are doing presently, and in the future. If you don't know what you want from life, what do you think you will get? Surely, you will get absolutely nothing! Be sure about what you want from life, and doubly sure of what you have to give in return. Examine most carefully the things you desire most, for you shall get nothing tangible without sacrifice. Wisdom consists in knowing what not to want, as well as what to want. Don't be afraid to aim high when choosing your life's goal, for no matter how high you aim, your achievements may still fall below it. Keep so busy going after what you want that you have no time to fear what you don't want. If you don't know what you want do not say you never had a chance.

Co-operation

Willing co-operation produces enduring power, while forced co-operation end in failure. No man can succeed and remain successful without the friendly Co-operation of others. Co-operation must start at the head of a department if it is expected at the other end. Ditto for efficiency. Friendly co-operation is never any part of the devil's work. He, the devil is busy working on the other side. Remember that no one can hurt your feelings without your co-operation and willingness. Friendly co-operation will get a man more, than unfriendly agitation in any marketplace.

Courage

Courage is often one jump ahead of fear. The man who complains that he never had a chance, probably does not have the courage to take a chance. If you don't know something, summon courage to admit it and you will be well on the road toward learning.

Criticism

One way to avoid criticism is to do nothing and be nobody. The world will then not bother you. Never fear unjust criticism but be sure it is unjust. If inventors feared criticisms, we would still be traveling by ox-cart and horse; and also wearing primitive clothing. Don't be afraid of criticism but be prepared to accept it if you have a better idea to offer. If you cannot stand criticism, you may as well not begin anything new. If you can't take criticism, you have no right to dish it out to others. Before you start criticizing, you had better do a little softening up by praise. Praise more freely than you criticizes, if you wish to be popular.

Deeds

If you are really great, you will let others discover this fact from your deeds. Count that day lost, whose descending sun finds you with no good deeds done. The only safe way to boast is by constructive deeds, not by mere words. Self-praise is a credit only when it consists of deeds helpful to others, and not of mere words.

Deeds, not words, are the greatest means of self-praise. The man who thinks he can buy his way into heaven with money alone, may regret that he didn't convert it into good deeds instead. It is not the epitaph on your tombstone that matter, but the record of your deeds that may perpetuate your name after death. Faith is a combination of thoughts and deeds.

Definiteness of Purpose

A man without a definite major purpose in life is as helpless as a ship without a compass, because it will be tossed about on the sea of life. All riches consist in the habit of clear thinking. If you have no major purpose in life, your minor purpose will amount to nothing but a scant existence. A rudderless ship and a purposeless man are eventually stranded on desert sand.

Willpower is the outgrowth of definiteness of purpose expressed through persistent action based on personal initiative. Living without a definite major purpose in life promises nothing but a scant living. If you have no major purpose, you are drifting toward certain failure. Constancy of purpose is the first principle of success. Honesty and hard work are commendable traits of character, but they will never make a success of the man who does not guide them toward a major definite purpose.

Education and learning

Education means development of the mind from within the individual; it will enable him to take his problems apart and put them to work, for him, not against him. All education is self-acquired since no-one can educate another.

An educated person is not necessarily someone who has all the knowledge, but the one who knows where to get it when he needs it. Knowledge is not just power; it is only potential power that becomes real through its effective usage over time.

Knowledge, when intelligently used, attracts greater knowledge. The more you learn about your job, the more you may earn from your job. The person who learns while he earns is being paid to go to school. Knowledge is useless until it is transformed into benefit through positive action.

Effective Speech

Speak gently and you will not need to weigh your words so carefully; the man who speaks gently is heard further. Remember, every word you speak gives someone a chance to find out how much – or how little you know. Carelessly expressed words often have an embarrassing rebound, watch what you say. Not what you say that matter, but the way you say it counts. Think what you please but be careful how you express your thoughts.

Enthusiasm

Where enthusiasm is a habit, fear and worry do not hang around. If you are without enthusiasm, you are without a definite major purpose. A man without enthusiasm is like a car without fuel. Enthusiasm starts the wheel of imagination turning around. Enthusiasm often makes dull conversation interesting. The happiest men are those who have learned to mix play with their work and bind the two together with enthusiasm.

Going the Extra Mile

A good fisherman goes out of his way to bait his hook with what fish prefer. This is a good tip for those who wish to succeed. Remember, every time you go the extra mile you place someone under obligation to you.

Only those who have the habit of going the second mile, ever find the end of the rainbow. Every time you influence another person to do a better job, you benefit him and increase your own value. You cannot make everyone to like you, but you can rob them of a sound reason for disliking you. The man, who does more than he is paid for, is sooner or later

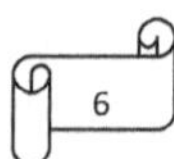

paid willingly for more than what he does. This is the actual meaning of **going the extra mile**. He is richest who gives most in service to others.

Failure

Many men have found opportunities in failure and adversity, which they could not recognize in more favorable circumstances. Success requires no explanations; failures must be doctored with alibis. Drifting without aim or purpose, is the first major cause of failure. Edison failed ten thousand times before perfecting the modern electric lamp. The average man would have quit at the first failure, don't worry if you fail once. That is why there are many "average" men, and only one Mr. Edison, the inventor. There is a vast difference between failure and temporary defeat; a man is never a failure until he accepts defeat as permanent and then quits trying. Most failures could have been converted into successes if someone had held on for another minute or made one more effort. Success often attracts success, but failure attracts failure because of the law of harmonious attraction. The man who tries to get something for nothing generally winds up getting nothing for something. Think about this. If you don't know why you failed, you are no wiser than when you began. What is the assurance that you will not fail again?

Fairness

Don't overlook small details, remember that the universe and all that is in it are made from atoms, the smallest known particles of matter. The best way to start getting favors is to start handing out favors to people.

Faith

Faith is a state of mind that often makes the word "impossible" obsolete. Faith is born of **definiteness of purpose** operating in a positive mental attitude. Faith will not bring you what you desire, but it will show you the way to go after it for yourself. Faith never diminishes through use, but it increases thereby. No man can destroy your faith in anything unless you give consent. The greatest of all miracles is the power of simple faith. Faith needs a foundation on which to stand but fear exists without a base. Have faith in your ability to succeed, also have faith in God to help you.

Fear

Fear is the devil's greatest weapon, and man's greatest enemy. Fear is the costliest of all human emotions, although most fears have no foundation in facts. Men with clear conscience seldom fear anything. Don't temporize with fear, just go ahead and kill it. Every bargain based on fear or force is a bad bargain for one who drives it. Hope and fear don't travel together. Fear is bombastic; faith works in silence; but it works. When the two meet head-on, faith always is the master of fear.

Friends

A friend is someone who knows all about you, and still respects you. Friendship needs frequent expression to remain alive. It recognizes faults in friends but does not speak of them. If you must let someone down, be sure it is not a friend who helped you get up

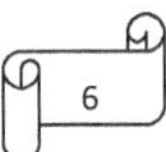

when you were down. Friends are to be grown, not taken for granted. The man, who calls on his friends only when he needs something, soon finds himself without friends. If you wish to have a friend, be a friend yourself.

Habit of good Health

Ripe fruits and raw vegetables constitute a healthful diet of which you can never over-eat. When you feel sluggish, try nature's doctor. Just quit eating food until you are hungry again. Proper diet and elimination of body wastes will serve better than an apple a day to keep the doctor away. Watch your eating habits and save a doctor's bill.

Don't try to cure a headache; it is better to cure the thing that caused it. A big appetite does not always lead to sound health. Pills will not cure toxic poisoning, but plenty of water will. Keep your mind on your physical ills and you will always be sick. Ditto for health!

Handicapped

If you become discouraged, think about Helen Keller who, although deaf, dumb and blind made a good living by writing books, to inspire her more fortunate fellow men and women. A blind boy paid his way to a Master's Degree in the university by taking notes in Braille system, writing them out on a typewriter, and selling copies to his classmates who had stronger eyes but weak ambition. The man who starts at the top is greatly handicapped because, then he can only move in one direction – downward if care is not taken.

Happiness

Happiness can be multiplied by sharing it with others, without diminishing the original source. It is the one asset which increases when it is given away. A smile is a little thing that may produce big results. Happiness is found in doing – not merely in possessing it. You can't find happiness by robbing another of it. Ditto for economic security. The man who gives freely of happiness always has a big stock of it on hand.

Harmony

There is harmony throughout the universe, and in everything except human relationships. If you cannot agree with one another, you can at least refrain from quarrelling with him on that account. The orderliness of the world, and of natural laws gives evidence that they are under control of a universal plan. The man who inspires harmony in human relationships goes up; but the man who stirs up friction goes down. The order is never reversed.

Mutual confidence is the foundation of all satisfactory human relationships. The most important job is that of learning how to negotiate with others and without friction. Anything that disturbs harmony amongst men is apt to have originated with those who profit from mistrust.

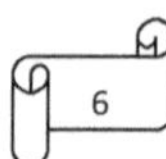

Hope and Encouragement

Time is the greatest of all doctors. If given a chance, it can cure most of the ills that men worry and complain about. If you look around, you can always find someone who is worse off than yourself. So, be grateful that you are not in his shoes. Misfortune seldom tangles with someone whose constant companion or bodyguards are hope and faith. When hope dies, opportunity seldom attends the funeral, but hope and fear don't travel together. Hope and faith are the willing servants of successful men; but opulence without effort is a hope without fulfillment. When things become so bad that they cannot become worse, they usually begin to get better. Clothes may not make a man, but they can go a long way towards giving him a favorable start.

Human Relationships

Harmony in human relationship is a man's greatest asset. When you can't win, you can at least give a smile. Don't permit anyone to rob you of your share. Jealousy is temporary **insanity**. You cannot be perfect, but you can be honest. The man who builds a house always gets more for his work than the man who **tears it down**.

It takes more than a title and executive desk or table to make on an **executive**. Your job will do for you no more than you can do for it. If you are looking for trouble, someone will be meddlesome enough to help you find it. Your **reputation** is made by others, but your **character** is made by you. Never mind what you did in the past; but what are you doing now and in the future?

Revenge is the trait of the primitive man. Discourtesy to a subordinate is a sure sign of an inferiority complex. Ability is greater than money because it can neither be lost nor stolen. Hatred and justice cannot occupy a small mind at the same time, because one must give way to the other.

Imagination

Imagination is the workshop of the soul, where-in is shaped all the plans and actions leading to individual achievements. Your job and achievements will never be any bigger than your imagination makes it. Imagination is the mind's exercise, its challenges, its adventure and the mind's workshop. It creates, visualizes, foresees and generates ideas. <u>Man's greatest gift is his thinking mind</u>. Think thoroughly before you take action to avoid regrets. Also think outside the box for effective solution to nagging issues.

Personal Initiative

Personal initiative is a trait much admired, and if carried out with discretion and logic can very quickly put one ahead of the crowd. Personal initiative is self-confidence in action. If you are moving toward a definite goal, it speeds your journey. Initiative built on a definite understanding of what must be achieved, puts one in harmony with those around him and with the universe around him. It is a self-reliant demonstration of which seldom goes unnoticed by those in authority.

Mental Attitude

The quality and quantity of service you render, plus the mental attitude in which you render it determines the amount of pay you get, and the sort of job you hold. The man with <u>negative mental attitude</u> is like an electro-magnet that attracts steel filings. No man is ever rewarded with promotion because of a <u>negative mental attitude</u>. It is far better to imitate a successful person than to envy him. Quick promotions are not always the most enduring. A mind is not greater than the thoughts that dominate his mind, a closed mind stumbles over the blessings of life without recognizing them. Remember, your mental limitations are your own making.

Master – Mind

The mind grows only through use and becomes stale through idleness. A man is not greater than the thoughts that dominate the mind; ensure that only positive thoughts inhabit your mind. A <u>closed mind</u> stumbles over the blessings of life without recognizing them; always keep an open mind on all things to ensure success. Take possession of your own mind, and you soon make life pay off on your own terms.

Remember that the mind grows stronger through use. Struggle makes power. A quick decision denotes an alert mind. Henry Ford's mind was precisely like every other normal mind, but he used his mind to think with. He did not harbor any fear, doubt and self imposed limitations. Same applies to other great minds, thinkers and dreamers.

Control your own mind, and you may never be controlled by the mind of another person. A man's progress begins in his own mind and ends in the same place if properly used. The mind serves best when it is used most often. It never becomes tired, but sometimes become "bored" with the sort of food it gets. Your mind is your own, and so is the responsibility as to how you use it; know your own mind and you will be as wise as the sages. If you know your own mind, you will know enough to keep it always positive for optimum results.

Loyalty

Two things money cannot buy are love and friendship. These are gifts of the gods and have no fixed price. One great lesson to be learned from a dog is that of <u>enduring loyalty</u>. The dog that does not wag its tail when its master comes home had better be looking for another master.

If all men had the loyalty and gratitude of dogs, this world would have been a pretty and fair world. The man who owns a good dog is never without a friend, because of its loyalty. In heaven's name, don't ever bite the hand that feeds you – for friends must be grown to order, and not taken for granted.

The Mind and Mental Attitude

The physical body is a mechanical house in which the mind dwells. No one has yet discovered the limitations of the power of **his own mind**. A negative mind never attracts

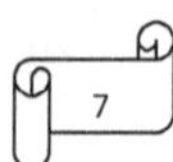

happiness or material success, but it will attract their opposites. Good manners begin with a positive mental attitude.

Every brain is both a broadcasting station and a receiving station for the vibrations of thought. A well-disciplined mind recognizes but few limitations. Your mind belongs to you exclusively. Take possession of it, direct it to specific usage, and make life pay off on your own terms. A man's likes and dislikes come back to him from unexpected sources and are often **greatly multiplied**. If your mind can make you sick, remember that it can also make you well. Your true age is determined by your mental attitude, not the years that you have lived. One optimist may wield more constructive influence than a thousand pessimists. Most illnesses begin with a negative mind. Men with positive mental attitudes (PMA) are never in a rut, they are never discouraged nor defeated. Your own mental attitude is your own boss; hold unto it always. If you are not on good terms with your conscience, take time out and read the Sermon on the Mount, (Matthew chapter 5:1-12), you will derive a lot of benefit from that sermon.

Opportunity

Opportunity has a queer way of following the person who can recognize it and is ready to embrace it. The man who is not quick to see his limitations, generally is slow in seeing his opportunities. Another man's mistakes may be a rich field of opportunity for you, if you know what caused his mistakes.

If you are an able-bodied Nigerian, don't ever admit that the world has not given you opportunities for self-improvement. It all depends on your own mental conditioning; for there are opportunities everywhere you turn to. Key yourself up with expectations, and opportunity may just give the key a turn for the better. Opportunity will let you down if you are not strong enough to hold it up. If you could see an opportunity as quickly as you see the faults of others, you would soon become rich. When you close the door of your mind to negative thoughts, then the doors of opportunity open to you. Opportunities often knock only to find no-one around to grab it. A resourceful person will always make opportunity fit his needs.

Opportunity wastes no effort looking for the person who is wasting his time through idleness or destructive action. Opportunity will not interest itself in the person who is not interested in it. Opportunities are captured only by those who dare to attack, not those who merely wait for it to come.

Opinions

Most opinions are mere hopeful wishing, not the result of careful analysis of facts. It is more beneficial to ask intelligent questions than it is to offer free opinions which have not been requested. Never express an opinion unless you can explain how you came by it. Your opinions may be safer if you don't express it as a fact. If your opinions are worth anything, why give them away so freely. Just tell me the facts and omit the opinions.

Organized Thinking (or Accurate Thinking)

You are where you are and what you are because of the food you eat, and the thoughts you think. Some nuggets of thought are worth more than nuggets of gold. Ponder the fact that one has complete control over but one thing, and that is the power over one's thoughts. It may do no good to "stop, look and listen", unless you also think.

If you are truly smart, you should know when to stop talking and start listening. Think your way through, then push the body through.

Peace of Mind

A man who is at peace with himself is also at peace with the world. Unless you have peace of mind, you are not a free person. Nothing that causes a person to worry is worth what his worry costs him, in peace of mind and physical health.

Don't take yourself too seriously if you wish to get any joy out of life. Get on good terms with yourself and see how quickly others get on good terms with you. If you are not at peace with yourself, you cannot be at peace with others. If you are truly at peace with yourself, you will never be at war with others.

Personal Initiative

The most important job goes to the man who can get it done without passing the buck or coming back with excuses or alibis. Act on your own initiative but be prepared to assume full responsibilities for your acts. Anything that stifles personal initiative is definitely an enemy of individual achievement.

Pleasant Personality

Men will like you better when you greet them with a smile, instead of a frown. <u>You will always be welcome if you bring a smile with you and leave your worries at home. Life never is sweet to the man who is sour on the world.</u> When you can't win, you can at least grin. Three little words "if you please", - carry the power of great charm.

I have heard it said that they never mistrust a man who whistles or sings when he works. One thing that gets the goat of an angry person is a smile, when he expects a frown.

Prayer

The greatest and most restful of all prayers are those offered as gratitude for blessings we already have. It is better to give thanks for the blessings we already have, before praying for more blessings. The art of being grateful for the blessings you already possess is of itself the most profound form of worship, an incomparable gem of prayer

<u>Prayers expressed with fear or doubt always produce only negative results. Whenever you pray, do it with confidence and faith for effective results.</u>

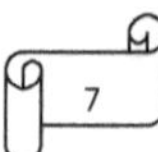

Procrastination

Procrastination is the bad habit of putting off till tomorrow something that should have been done the day before yesterday. The habitual procrastinator always is an expert creator of alibis. Suspense is the child of indecision, and it is the first cousin of procrastination. It is also the "pet" that keeps many people in poverty.

Realities

The five known realities of the entire universe are time, space, matter, energy, and the intelligence that gives orderliness. There are no such realities as good or bad luck. Everything has a cause that produces appropriate effects. There is no such reality as passive faith. Action is the first requirement of all faith, words alone, will not serve. The only permanent thing in the entire universe is change. Nothing is ever the same for two consecutive days. Today's dreams become tomorrow's realities. Do not belittle the practical dreamer, for he is the forerunner of civilization.

Self-Confidence and Self-Respect

Self-confidence may be mistaken for <u>egotism</u>, if it is not accompanied by humility of the heart. Too much self-confidence often inspires too little caution. Self-respect is the best means of getting the respect of others. Sound character always begins with keen self respect. It always takes more than a loud voice to gain respect for authority.

Self-Control

An educated man is one who has learned how to get what he wants without violating the rights of others. Before trying to master others, be sure you are the master of yourself. Develop your ego but keep your foot on its neck. Independence starts with self-dependence. Hotheads don't produce cool thoughts. Hatred may not injure others, but the damage it does to the hater is **inescapable**. When you get yourself under **complete control**, you can be your own boss.

Self-Discipline

Self-discipline is the first rule of all successful leadership. True Wisdom begins with self-understanding based on self-discipline. You can't control other men's acts, but you can surely control your mental reaction to their acts, and that is what counts to you. Have you ever tried to be angry while smiling? Try it! When angry, try whistling for three minutes before speaking, and observe how your anger will take on the quality of reason. Self-discipline makes discipline from the outside un-necessary and when you get yourself under complete control, you can be your own boss.

Silence

Silence has one major advantage; it gives no-one a clue as to what your next move shall be. Silent thought is more powerful than spoken words. Sometimes the man whom you think that you have beaten by talk, has outwitted you by silence.

Sleep

When you do not know what to do with your problem, try sleeping on it for a night or so, before taking further action.

A friendly conscience is a mighty good cure for sleeplessness. If you cannot sleep, have a look at your stomach, or have a confidential talk with your conscience.

Sound Physical Health

Eat right, think right, sleep right, and play right and you can save the doctor's bill for your vacation money. If you think you are sick, then you are. When you begin looking for symptoms of illness, the disease itself will soon appear. Searching for symptoms often lead to physical and mental illness.

Stubbornness

Differences of opinion without tolerance, generally turns out to be only stubbornness. Plain stubbornness is often mistaken for "pride"; avoid it, if you wish to succeed.

Sub-Conscious Mind

The record of every person's life is indelibly recorded in his/her sub-conscious mind. The sub-conscious mind often works out one's greatest problems when the conscious mind is asleep. Keep your conscious mind fixed on what you desire, and your sub-conscious mind will un-erringly guide you to it.

Success

Money may not make a man a success, but it does give him a mighty good reputation. The greatest of all success rules is: - Do unto others as you would want others to do unto you. No man ever becomes so successful that he does not appreciate a kindly word of commendation for work well done.

The greatest of all schools is popularly known as the "University of Hard Knocks". The surest way to promote yourself is to help others get ahead. The successful leader makes decisions quickly but changes them slowly, if they must be changed.

Most successful men in the higher bracket of success did not strike their best stride until they passed the age of forty. The man or woman, who has only time for gossip and slander is too busy to pursue success in any endeavor.

Anyone can stand poverty, but few can stand success and riches, because those who work hard always succeed. Success that comes easily is apt to go quickly too. No one can keep you down except yourself. Defeat does not discourage the man who **knows** he is right. Man, seldom ever begins to succeed in the higher brackets of success until he is past forty, mainly because most of his early years are spent in un-learning things that are not true.

Success-Consciousness

The conscience speaks, not in audible words but through that small voice from within us. If your conscience is not clear, you had better start house-cleaning from within yourself. An apology is a healthy indication that a man is still on speaking terms with his own conscience.

Tactfulness

There can never be any harm in speaking about other people provided you speak of their good qualities. When you don't know anything well to say about a man, just button-up your lips and you will feel better. You can get close to a man by the simple process of taking a keen sincere interest in what he is doing. Merited praise will gain reciprocal interest from any man. If you must talk about your good qualities, try not to cover too much territory.

A truly big man never tries to impress others with his bigness, and never tries to "keep up with the Joneses" It is better to request a man to perform a service than it is to order him to perform it. When the other fellow's facial expression looks pained, it is time to stop talking or change the conversation.

Teamwork

A good football team consists in harmonious co-ordination of effort more than in individual skills.

When you ask someone to do something, it may help both him and you if you tell him

- what to do;
- why he should do it;
- when he should do it;
- where he should do it; and □ how he may best do it.

Temper

A temper is good to have, provided one does not try to give it to someone else. Temperament is a state of mind consisting of two parts – "temper" and one-part mental energy. When you lose your temper, you will be better off not to go back to find it. Hot heads don't produce cool thoughts. When you become so angry that you don t know what to do, it will be safer to do nothing than to remain calm and cool.

Thoughts

If a man gave spoken expression to every thought that came into his mind, he would have no friends. Hot heads don't produce cool thoughts, always remain cool headed, no matter the situation. Thoughts are contagious. Therefore, be careful of the sort of thoughts you release. Release only positive thoughts always.

Time

Time is a wonderful healer. It tends to equalize both good and evil, and also rights the wrongs of the world. Nothing is impossible with time. Tell me how you use your "spare" time, and I will tell you what and where you will be in ten years' time. You will find time for all your needs if you have time properly organized. The most profitable time any man spends is that for which he is not directly paid. The man who wastes his own time may be no less a thief than the man who steals another people's property. There has always been a shortage of men who get the job done on time without excuses or grumbling. The length of time a man sticks to a job is a pretty accurate measure of his dependability, reliability or consistency.

Don't waste your time on the man who forms his opinion before he examines the evidence. Time will cure worries which respond to no other treatment. Indecision and lack of a major purpose are the greatest of all thieves of time. The most beneficial use of time is that which one devotes to silent meditation when searching for guidance from within himself.

Time spent in silent thought may yield fabulous riches through the creation of sound ideas. When there is no work for your hand to perform, let your mind be employed so that even a second of time shall not be wasted. Live each day as if it were your last, and you will develop a keen respect for time. When defeat overtakes you, don't put all your time on counting your losses. Save some of it to look for your gains, and you may find your gains to be greater than your losses.

Some mistakes can be corrected, but not the mistake of wasted time. When time goes, it has gone forever. Don't cry over spilled milk. If you cannot forgive, don't ask to be forgiven, for you will be wasting precious time. The use of one's time determines the space one occupies in the world. Time, the great universal doctor, can cure all human ills, and most of them very quickly too. Remember there is always an end for everything, except time and space. Most misfortunes are the results of misused time. The poet cries, "Backward, turn backward, oh time in your flight". But he cries in vain, for time flows only ahead, it cannot wait or turn backward.

Will-Power

Anyone can quit when the going is tough, but a thorough-bred person never quits until he wins the race. Victory is always possible for the person who refuses to stop fighting. Nature yields her most profound secrets to the person who is determined to uncover them.

The most interesting thing about a postage stamp is the persistence with which it sticks to its job.

Wishing

If I had one wish, and it could be granted for the asking, I would ask for more wisdom from God. The scientist is the only person who does no hopeful wishing and accepts all

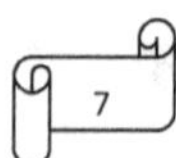

the facts as he finds them. If I had one wish that could be granted, it would be for more wisdom with which to enjoy the many blessings which God has granted humanity. If wishes were horses, even beggars would ride but it is not easy to acquire horses by merely Wishing.

Traits of Character

Dependability is the first foundation stone of good character. Your reputation is what people think you are, but your character is that which you are. Every thought a man release becomes a permanent part of his character. Sound character is a man's greatest asset, because it provides the power with which he may ride the emergencies of life instead of going down under them. Pick out someone whom you admire and imitate him or her closely as you can. This is hero worship, but it improves character. Boastfulness generally is an admission of inferiority complex; it is practiced only by little minds. Profanity is a sign of inadequate vocabulary or un-sound judgment, or both.

Money is either a good or bad influence, according to the character of the, person who possesses it. No man is so good that there is no bad in him, and no man is so bad that he has no good in him. Honesty is a spiritual quality that cannot be evaluated in terms of money. Attend well to your character and your reputation will look out for itself. The man with sound character generally does no Worrying over his reputation.

Bankers often lend money on character, but seldom on reputation alone, for they have learned that not all reputations are deserved.

Worry

Worry and success simply cannot live together in the same house. Success-consciousness is a death warrant for Mr. Worry. Never stop to think about your worries, for they will catch up with you quickly enough unless you outrun them.

Before worrying about how to get more pay, try thinking how you can do a better job and you may not need to worry much again. When enthusiasm comes in at the front door, worry runs out through the back door. Worry thrives on self-pity, do not give room for it to thrive in your own life.

Let the **other fellow** do the worrying if he has no better sense of purposeful engagement. Never listen to a doubting Thomas unless you are willing to become one, for doubt is a contagious disease if you allow it into your life. Most worries are not half as serious as their owners think they are. If you have time to worry, you haven't enough time to succeed in your job. Worries generally go to where they are most welcome.

Old man worry's relatives are: - fear, ill-health, ill temper, jealousy, selfishness, bad Judgment, indifference, procrastination, poverty, envy, premature old age, and discouragement. What a flock of negative traits. If you are too busy to visit with worries, they will be too discouraged to hang around your abode.

Only the weak crave sympathy! Forget your worries, and most of them will slap back by forgetting you finally.

Responsibility

High wages and the capacity to assume responsibilities are two things that belong together. Big pay and little responsibility are circumstances that are seldom found together. Don't cover the other fellow's job if you are not prepared to accept the responsibility that goes with it. If you do a job in another man's way, he takes the responsibility. But if you do it your own way, you must take the responsibility for the outcome.

The privilege of bringing children into the world carries with it the responsibility of teaching them the fundamentals of sound character.

Tone of Voice

Remember the tone of your voice often conveys more accurately what is in your mind than do your words.

Learning from Adversity

Before opportunity crowns a man with great success, it usually tests him out through adversity to see what sort of mettle he is made of. If you don't want your life to be "messed up", don't fool around with those who messed up theirs. When adversity overtakes you, it will pay you to be thankful it was not worse, instead of Worrying over your misfortune. You never know your real friends until adversity

Overtakes you, and you need financial co-operation from people. If life gives you a lemon, don't complain, but convert it into lemonade and sell it to those who are thirsty from constantly complaining about life's problems.

Liberty and Freedom

No man is free until he learns to do his own thinking and gains the courage to act on his own personal initiative. Thinking accurately makes a man free, but nothing else does. No man is free who holds a grudge against another person, for he is under bond to his own emotions. Don't be too hard on the "boss", for you may be a "boss" yourself someday.

High taxes with plenty of freedom are more desirable than no taxes without freedom. Freedom and fear cannot co-exist in any person's life, for a free man fears nothing except God. No man can be entirely free until he is entirely honest with himself.

Love

Love is just a game to an old bachelor, but it is a tonic to an old maid. There is something good about any man who is loved by his dog and his family, for they know him as he is. Only one thing will attract love, and that is love. Love, courtesy, and friendship are three priceless assets that cannot be purchased with money and **must be given away** before they become valid. Poets may rave about "love in a cottage", but others know that love goes out through the back door when poverty knocks at the front door.

Ideas

Just omit your opinions and give me the facts so I may form my own opinions, and you may serve me better. An opinion is no sounder than the person offering it. If you have a better way of doing anything, your idea or ideas may be worth a substantial fortune.

Life Insurance

Life insurance helps to kill the fear of poverty in old age. A man's love for his family can be pretty accurately measured by the amount of life insurance he carries for their protection. The man who spends all he earns will die a pauper if he neglects to carry life insurance. No man should go into debt for anything greater than the amount of life insurance he carries. You don t have to do more than you are paid for, but you can push yourself ahead mighty fast by doing it **voluntarily**.

Judging and Justice

Don't judge the entire church by its worst members. All wheat or corn is surrounded by chaff. Would you take a chance of being judged in heaven by the same rules that you judge your fellowmen?

Justice keeps an accurate record of **all debits and credits**, and it balances its books with regularity, if not with speed. Justice has the uncanny habit of catching up with people when they are least prepared for it.

Law of Compensation

The man, who does no more than he is paid for, has no real basis for requesting more pay because he is already getting all he is earning.

The man who does more than he is paid for is sooner or later paid willingly for more than he does. If you are looking for trouble, someone will be meddlesome enough to help you find it. Some men appear to be "allergic" to honest work, but opportunity is equally allergic to them. Remember that most troubles men get into, overtake them when they are in bad company or at places where they should not be.

The man who deliberately gets in the way of opportunity by being on the job all the time, sooner or later is crowned by opportunity. Henry Ford became rich, not from the sale of Ford cars but from the service he rendered through his cars. Do your job as if you were your own boss, and sooner or later you will be! Don't be satisfied with being good at your job. Be the best, and you will soon be indispensable. The law of compensation is not always swift, but it is as sure of operation as the setting of the sun.

Everyone needs a blue print by which to build his life. The great German Philosopher, Goethe set forth some principles for having a well-balanced life. Goethe's creed may give you the basis of a blue-print which will help you make life pay off on your own terms, without violating the rights of others. A daily creed helps one to keep before him or her a clear picture of the person one desires to become. It helps give him the power of faith to meet and overcome obstacles along the way. Goethe's creed goes as follows: - I desire: -

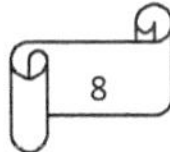

- Health enough to make work a pleasure;
- Wealth enough to support my needs;
- Strength enough to battle difficulties and overcome them; □ Patience enough to toil until some good has been accomplished.
- Grace enough to confess my sins and forsake them.
- Charity enough to see the good in my neighbors.
- Love enough to move me to be useful and helpful to others.
- Faith enough to make real the things of God; and
- Hope enough to overcome all fears concerning the future.

Henry Ford's Magical Faith

His biographer wrote about Henry Ford in the following language:

"Machines are to a mechanic, what books are to a writer. He gets ideas from them, and if he has any brain, he will apply these ideas. This was Henry Ford's philosophy – he was surrounded with machines.

Genius, they say is infinite patience, success also demands patience. Those who are tempted to give up after a few months, or a few years should be encouraged by this man's tenacity, which I call **Henry Ford's magical faith**, because he refused to recognize that there are impossibilities in the world." He said that impossibility is temporal but impossibility also belongs to God alone. He did not believe in the word impossible.

Culled from: Succeed and Grow Rich Through Persuasion by Dr. Napoleon Hill and E. Harold Keown, Fawcett Publications, Inc. USA.

CHAPTER TEN

YOUR ATTITUDE AND MOTIVATION IS KEY

POPE FRANCIS: ON HAPPINESS AND SUCCESS

You can have flaws (weakness in character), you can be anxious, and even be angry, but do not forget that your life is the greatest enterprise in the world. Only you can stop it from going burst (or braking). Many people appreciate you, admire you and love you. Remember that to be happy is not to have a sky without a storm, a road without accidents, work without fatigue, and relationships without disappointment.

To be happy is to find strength in forgiveness;

Hope is battles, security when you are in the state of fear and love in discord. It is not only to enjoy the smile,

But also, to reflect on the sadness.

It is not only to celebrate the success, but to learn lessons from the failures.

It is not only to feel happy with the applause,

But to be happy in anonymity.

Being happy is not a fatality of destiny,

But an achievement for those who can travel within themselves as they succeed in life.

To be happy is to stop feeling like a victim and become your destiny author. It is to cross deserts, yet to be able to find an oasis in the depths of our soul.

It is to thank God for every morning, for the miracle of life. Being happy is not being afraid of your own feelings.

It is to be able to talk about you. It's having the courage to hear or say "no" at the appropriate time.

It is confidence in the face of criticism, even when unjustified. It is to kiss your children, pamper your parents, to live poetic moments with friends and relations even when they hurt us.

To be happy is to let live the creature that lives in each of us, free, joyful and simple.

It is to have maturity to be able to say, "I made mistakes". It is to have the courage to say "I am sorry".

It is to have the sensitivity to say " I need you".

It is to have the ability to say, "I love you".

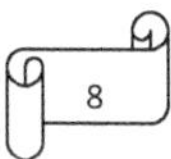

May your life become a garden of opportunities for happiness and success.

That in spring, may it be a lover of joy –

In Winter, a lover of wisdom.

And when you make a mistake, start all over again.

For only then will you be in love with life.

You will find that to be happy is not to have a perfect life. But use the tears to irrigate tolerance.

Use your losses to train patience; use your mistakes to sculpture serenity.

Use pain to plaster pleasure; use obstacles to open windows of intelligence and success.

Never give up! Never give up on people who love you!

Never give up on happiness, for life is an incredible show.

Have a prosperous New Year, 2018.

The Pontiff, Pope Francis, Vatican City, Rome.

The Sunday Sun issue of Jan. 18th 2018.

SECTION B

CHAPTER ELEVEN

BRIEF HISTORY OF NIGERIAN BANKS

It was in the year 1892 that banking activities first started in Nigeria with the opening of a branch of the African Banking Corporation in Lagos. The bank was incorporated in Britain, and owned by Elder Demister Company, a shipping firm based in Liverpool. The principal aim of the bank at the time was to service British trading interests in Nigeria, such as the Royal Niger Company and other similar companies. Owing to initial difficulties, the bank wound up its activities, and another bank, the Bank of British West Africa Limited, (BBWA) was established in 1894 to take over the activities of the former one.

The BBWA Limited opened its first Lagos branch in the same year, and later spread to other parts of Nigeria owing to later political developments in the country, the bank changed name several times and is presently known as the First Bank of Nigeria Limited. (now a Public Limited Liability Company Plc).

The second bank to establish in Nigeria was Barclays Bank DCO (Dominion, Colonial and Overseas) which opened its first branch in Lagos in 1917. The bank later changed its name to Union Bank of Nigeria and opened up branches in many parts of the country. The two expatriate banks mentioned above were joined in 1949 by another foreign bank, the British and French Bank (now UBA – United Bank for Africa Limited). The above named bank took its root from another bank established by the French in other West African countries. The banking scheme continued to be monopolized by foreign banks who between 1949 and 1954 tried to beat a rumored indigenous banking initiative by a pending legislation.

However following discriminations suffered by Nigerians in the hands of these foreign banks, some patriotic Nigerians grouped themselves for the purpose of breaking the monopoly as a result of which the National Bank of Nigeria was founded in 1933. With the Second World War coming to an end, there were increased economic activities, and no less than four indigenous banks were opened during the twenty months period between May 1945 and January 1947. However, only one of these banks, Agbonmagbe Bank (now Wema Bank Plc), is the only one surviving till date. The other banks died prematurely principally as a result of low capitalization, poor management and aggressive competition by expatriate banks. As a matter of fact, between 1947 and 1952, a total of 22 banks were registered in Nigeria according to a study conducted by the Central Bank of Nigeria, but most of them went into liquidation within four years.

Thus, the period from 1892 to 1952 were regarded by Central Bank authorities as a period of 'free-for-all' banking. This was because, at that time there were no licensing for banks nor regulations to restrict or control their operation in Nigeria. It was this state of affairs which led to many failures and consequent losses to depositors that promoted the setting up of the Paton Commission of inquiry to investigate the activities of banks and make recommendations.

As a result of the Commission's reports, the first banking legislation in Nigeria was enacted and called the Banking Ordinance of 1952. This ordinance was to serve as an important landmark between the period of non-regulated banking activities (or open banking era), and the introduction of modern regulated financial system in Nigeria. It also introduced vital regulations aimed at ensuring an orderly commercial banking system and preventing the emergence of unviable banks. The legislation thus limited the business of banking to only establishments validly licensed to engage in it.

11.1   THE PERIOD FROM 1956 TO 1986

While it might be appropriate to describe the period of 1892 to 1952 as one of "free-for all-banking"; the period from 1958 to 1986 could then be rightly called the years of regulated banking in Nigeria. This was a period mainly characterized by several banking and Foreign Exchange Acts. It is pertinent to mention here however, that the period of regulated banking activities which started in 1952, reached its climax in 1958 with the setting up of the Central Bank of Nigeria (CBN), as the country's apex bank (or regulatory authority) in the industry.

Right from inception, the Central Bank of Nigeria commenced the issuance of regular credit policy guidelines to the banking system. The first foreign exchange regulation was promulgated in 1962 (i.e., the Foreign Exchange Act of 1962). This act, for the first time tried to regulate the country's foreign exchange practices, but other banking regulations were to follow later. It is important to mention at this stage that the Banking Ordinance of 1952 was amended in 1958 and 1962; it was however replaced by the Banking Act of 1969. This Banking Act of 1969 also underwent some minor amendments in 1970, 1972 and 1974, but has remained the principal banking regulation in Nigeria until 1986 when the Structural Adjustment Program (SAP) was introduced by the Federal Government of Nigeria.

11.2   THE POST STRUCTURAL ADJUSTMENT PERIOD (SAP)

The advent of Structural Adjustment Program, (SAP) in Nigeria gave birth to a completely new era characterized by deregulation of the banking system.

Deregulation involved the systematic dismantling of regulatory controls and operational guidelines which were considered to have hindered orderly and systematic growth of banks in Nigeria. It brought with it a kind of revolution which made it fashionable for people to own banks in the country.

Deregulation gave room for the formation and licensing of numerous new commercial and merchant banks. Apart from allowing easy formation of banks, finance companies and bureau de-change were also granted permission to commence operations. Thus, with eight commercial banks and about 190 branch offices in 1960, there emerged no fewer than 124 commercial and merchant banks (with 2076 branches) as at the end of December, 1994 according to reports released by the Central Bank of Nigeria.

Deregulation of the banking industry in Nigeria appeared justified principally on the grounds and belief that there was need to remove complex administrative controls in the system, and to ensure greater reliance on the market mechanism.

The deregulation was intended to control obvious defects in the system which retarded growth and efficiency in credit delivery, and the intermediation role of the system. It has been further observed that after more than ten years since the introduction of financial deregulation as part of economic reform measures in the country, serious distortions have manifested itself in the macro economy with a large number of banks suffering from one form of banking distress or another. This cankerworm of distress has greatly affected banking habits and confidence, and also brought the system on the brink of collapse.

According to Central Bank of Nigeria Annual Report for 1994, out of a total of 124 (one hundred and twenty-four) Commercial and Merchants Banks, 57 (fifty-seven) were grappling with varying degree of distress, while 4 (four) had totally failed and liquidated entirely. Thereafter, it was reported that 15 (fifteen) more banks had been acquired by the apex regulatory body. This development became a source of serious concern and embarrassment both to the government, depositors and the investing public. The pertinent question being asked by all has therefore been, why did deregulation of the banking system become the scourge that led to the distress of the system? Nevertheless, worse news was yet to come regarding banking distress in Nigeria as time went on.

During the 1998 Federal Budget breakdown, the Minister of Finance announced that the Federal Government had finally listed a total of 26 (twenty-six) distressed banks for liquidation. The announcement thus ended the uncertainty over the number of financial institutions to be liquidated by the government. It was widely believed that the banks are those that were acquired by the Central Bank of Nigeria for ₦1.00 (one Naira) each in 1995.

With more than ₦19bn (Nineteen Billion Naira) deposits trapped in distressed banks, there is no doubt that deregulation has been greatly put in doubt. As a result of the foregoing therefore, scholars and banking/finance researchers felt the need to properly articulate the nature of distress and the causal factors. They also felt the need to ascertain if there is any close relationship with the failure of the Structural Adjustment Program (SAP) in Nigeria and the banking distress being witnessed presently. The result of their findings is expected to be published in due course and would aid policy formulators in taking future decisions affecting the Nigerian economy as a whole.

LIST OF LIQUIDATED BANKS

(AS ANNOUNCED BY THE MINISTER OF FINANCE)

	COMMERCIAL BANKS		MERCHANTS BANKS
1.	Allied Bank of Nig. Plc	1.	Abacus Merchant Bank Ltd
2.	Amicable Bank of Nig. Ltd	2.	ABC Merchant Bank Ltd
3.	Commerce Bank Ltd	3.	Century Merchant Bank Ltd
4.	Commercial Trust Bank Ltd	4.	Continental Merchant Bank Ltd

5.	Co-operative & Commerce Bank Ltd	5.	Crown Merchant Bank Ltd
6.	Credit Bank Limited	6.	Great Merchant Bank Ltd
7.	Highland Bank of Nig. Ltd	7.	Group Merchant Bank Ltd
8.	Lobi Bank of Nig. Ltd	8.	ICON Limited (Merchant Bankers)
9.	Mercantile Bank of Nig. Plc	9.	Merchant Bank of Africa Ltd
10.	North-South Bank Nig Plc	10.	Nigeria Merchant Bank Plc
11.	Pan-African Bank Ltd	11.	Prime Merchant Bank Ltd
12.	Pinnacle Commercial Bank Ltd	12.	Royal Merchant Bank Ltd
13.	Progress Bank of Nig. Plc	13.	Victory Merchant Bank Ltd

At independence in 1960, Nigeria had just one merchant bank in operation, i.e., Nigerian Acceptances Limited (later known as NAL Merchant Bank Ltd), but there were not less than 55 of them in operation (and 101 branch offices) during the period up to 31^{sst} December, 1991.

Also, more than 300 non-bank finance houses, over 60 Mortgage banks emerged during the period above-mention. Notable among the new entrants during the post-SAP – era is the Peoples Bank of Nigeria with 210 branches (and 508 Satellite Stations) as at the end of June, 1992.

The Community Banking Scheme also came on stream from early 1991, and as at the end of 1997 over 1,000 Community Banks were already in operation scattered in all the states across the Federation. Even insurance companies also flourished during the period. For instance, in 1921 there was only one in operation (i.e., Royal Exchange Insurance Co. Ltd.). But as at June 1992, the number rose to 96 with branches all over the country.

It could thus be seen that with the Structural Adjustment Program, there came a multiplicity and diversification of financial institutions (or boom) in the industry. This situation also gave rise to the emergence of more instruments of control and 'mediators. Among these were the Nigerian Deposit Insurance Corporation (NDIC), which is charged with the responsibility of insuring banks' deposits against failures. The NDIC set up in 1989, also has the duty (in collaboration with the Central Bank of Nigeria) of ensuring that banks observe sound and safe banking practices. This objective has to be achieved by effectively monitoring and supervising the banks in conjunction with the Central Bank of Nigeria. The establishment of NDIC appears to have instilled more confidence into the industry, as it allayed fears of possible collapse of the financial system as a result of the proliferation of banks. Other agencies or intermediaries which were established by the Federal Government as a result of the deregulation included the following: -

- The Securities and Exchange Commission (SEC) in 1988;

- The National Economic Reconstruction Fund (NERFUND), was established by Decree No. 2 of 1989 for the purpose of providing medium to long term financing to small and medium scaled production enterprise, and to act as a catalyst towards the stimulation of the rapid rise of real production enterprises in Nigeria;

- The Nigeria Export-Import Bank (NEXIM) was set up in 1991 for the promotion of Nigeria's import and export trade (but is lays greater emphasis of financing of exports);

- The Nigerian Urban Development Bank was floated by the Federal Government in 1992 for the purpose of enhancing rapid development of our urban centers. It lays greater emphasis on the provision of the much needed infrastructures such as roads, water supply, drainage, electricity, etc.

From the above account, it could thus be seen that the Structural Adjustment Program (SAP) and the deregulation of the financial system brought about a lot of changes (or revolution) into the Nigerian banking industry. Despite these upheavals, the general opinion is that the country is still under-banked. Proponents of this notion tend to buttress their arguments by pointing to undue delays in banks, inefficiency on the part of staff, frequent industrial unrest, and so on.

CHAPTER TWELVE

THE CENTRAL BANK OF NIGERIA

The Central Bank of Nigeria was established in 1958 as a result of the CBN Act of 1958, but the bank started operations on 1st July 1959. The Central Bank of Nigeria as the apex regulatory body for Nigerian financial system performs the following functions:

a) to ensure the relative stability of domestic prices by controlling the country's monetary system;

b) to maintain equilibrium in the country's international payments position;

c) promoting a rapid and sustainable rate of economic development in the country;

d) to issue legal tender currency in the country;

e) to maintain Nigeria's external reserves;

f) to safeguard the international value of Nigeria's currency;

g) to act as bankers and financial adviser to the Federal Government; and

h) to act as the bankers' bank, by acting as supervisor or regulator of all banks and financial institutions operating in the country.

The birth of the Central Bank of Nigeria brought a new dimension into the Nigerian banking scene. This is because, the Central Bank of Nigeria standing as both the apex and regulatory institution in the Nigerian banking industry, is required to possess statutory powers to regulate banking activities in the country. Its regulatory functions are achieved through the following means:

a) licensing of all banks operating in the country;

b) bank supervision and examination;

c) observance of banks' liquidity ratio;

d) ensuring that banks maintain minimum capital requirements;

e) maintenance of the country's reserves.

Other major functions carried out by the CBN include the following: -

a) To assist the Federal Government in determining an appropriate monetary and credit policy. It has the primary responsibility of formulating the country's monetary policies, as it makes proposals which are normally approved and incorporated into the yearly budget of the Federal Government of Nigeria;

b) It issues monetary Policy Circulars or CBN credit guidelines a few days after the release of the Federal Government's annual budget each year; These circulars or guidelines normally spell out the country's revised monetary regulations in full.

c) The CBN uses some instruments of control such as the discount rate system, direct regulation of interest rates, moral suasion, open market operations, reserve requirements, and direct control of credits through the use of prudential ratio and any other means of credit restrictions it deems fit.

d) It has responsibility of developing the Nigerian money and capital markets;

e) It manages the country's external reserves and has the responsibility for the administration of Nigeria's foreign exchange control system.

Initially, its regulatory functions were being carried out through the following means, namely:

Licensing, bank supervision and examination, minimum capital requirements, observance of liquidity ratios and the maintenance of reserves. However, it was the inevitable need for greater and better control of the Nigeria banking system which led to the enactment of various banking laws such as the CBN Act of 1958, the Banking Act of 1969 and other recent enactments such as: -

I.   the BOFID (Banks and Other Financial Institutions Decree of

1991),

II.   CAMD (Companies and Allied Matters Decree of 1990); and

III.   New Accounting Standards for Banks.

THE CENTRAL BANK OF NIGERIA AS THE SUPERVISOR AND REGULATOR OF BANKS IN NIGERIA

As we examine the role of the CBN in carrying out the above-stated functions, we find that the Banking Act of 1969 (S.20) empowers it to examine periodically, (under conditions of secrecy) the books and affairs of each and every licensed bank operating in the country.

The principal areas of bank regulations are: -

a) Adequacy of equity;

b) Liquidity and reserve requirements;

c) Maintenance of reserve fund;

d) Extension of credits;

e) Reporting and auditing requirements.

THE BANKING ACT 1969

The Banking Act 1969 (as amended) stipulated the following minimum capital requirements for banks: -

i. Indigenous banks   – ₦600,000

ii. Banks with foreign interest   – ₦1.5m

iii. Merchant Banks   – ₦2.3m

However, the Banking Act as it pertains to capitalization was amended in 1988 and the requirements for banks were as follows:

i. Commercial Banks   – ₦20 million

ii. Merchant Banks   – ₦12 million

The amounts specified above must be paid in full, and the Central Bank, after consultation with the Minister of Finance may stipulate the minimum ratio which licensed banks shall maintain between their paid up capital and all retained earnings on the one hand, and their loans and advances on the other. Any bank which fails to maintain this ratio may not apply its funds for payment of dividends to its shareholders (except with the approval of the Central Bank). It is important to note that banks are restricted in the ratio of their total lending to foreign business enterprises; and they are also required to allocate a percentage of their total lending to indigenous enterprises too.

There is also the provision that a proportion of the deposits generated in the rural areas, (30%) must be given out as loans/advances to those areas. How far these directives were being carried out was not actually known, but most banks were being penalized for failing to abide by this directive of the Central Bank of Nigeria, until recently when rural banking was abolished. Actually, with the advent of the Community Banking Scheme (which was initiated by the Federal Government in its 1990 Budget Speech), the rural banking scheme was a total failure.

Community Banks appear to have actually taken the place of the Rural Banking Scheme, because apart from providing banking services like the conventional commercial banks (though with some restrictions), they are also a very active agent in the economic development of the communities (which are primarily rural areas).

The Central Bank of Nigeria also imposed on banks, sectorial allocation of loans and advances in which case economics activities are divided into preferred, and less preferred sectors. Agriculture for instance falls into the preferred sector, (same with manufacturing industries); whilst general trading is placed under the less preferred sector. The CBN then proceeds to allocate certain percentage of the Bank's loans/advances to the various sectors above, but adequate sanctions are promptly meted out to banks who failed to observe the Sectorial Allocations as enunciated by the CBN. Also, an overall lending ceiling is usually imposed on the growth of the bank's loans and advances every year through the Central Bank's Monetary   Policy Circulars.

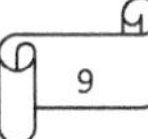

OTHER POWERS OF THE CENTRAL BANK OF NIGERIA

a) SUPERVISION OF BANKS

Section 20 of the Banking Act of 1969 (as amended in 1972), provided for the appointment of an officer of the Central Bank of Nigeria as Chief Bank Examiner (presently re-named Director of Banking Supervision). He or She is vested with the power to examine periodically the books and affairs of each and every licensed bank (under conditions of secrecy). The Director of Banking Supervision should be given free access to the books, accounts and vouchers of the bank; and also, satisfactory information and explanations must be given to the examiners whenever required.

Section 21 of the Banking Act 1969, also empowers the Central Bank to conduct a special examination (under conditions of secrecy) of the books and affairs of any licensed bank which is carrying on business in a manner detrimental to the interest of the depositors and other creditors.

The CBN also has powers to conduct special investigations if there is indication that a licensed bank has insufficient assets to cover its deposit and other liabilities to the public or is contravening the provisions of the Banking Act 1969.

There is also the provision that special investigation may be requested by holders of one third of the total number of shares issued and paid up, or depositors who hold not less than one half of the gross amount of the deposits of the bank. In this case however, applicants must submit evidence to the Federal Minister of Finance through the CBN in order to justify such examination. All costs and expenditures in connection with such examination must be borne by the applicants.

Special examination will also be conducted where a licensed bank suspends payments or informs the Minister of Finance or the Governor of the Central Bank of Nigeria of its intention to do so.

In a situation, for instance where a licensed bank considers that it is likely to be unable to meet its obligations, or it is about to suspend payments, it should inform the Central Bank of Nigeria in advance of its intention to do so. Any failure to make such report shall constitute an offence under the Banking Act of 1969.

Students are advised to familiarize themselves with the abovementioned Act since it forms one of the bedrocks of the Nigerian Banking System.

b) CENTRAL BANK'S RIGHT TO INTERVENE IN THE BANKING SYSTEM

Section 22 of the Banking Act 1969, provides that the Federal Minister of Finance, after considering the examination report submitted by the Central Bank of Nigeria, may take one or more of the following steps: -

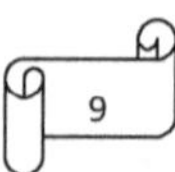

(i)   Order the bank to call a meeting of its directors immediately for the purpose of considering matters relating to the affairs of the bank as highlighted in the examination report, and to take necessary steps as the

Minister and Governor of the CBN may consider necessary to rectify the matter;

(ii)   Issue an order for immediate changes in its management personnel or structure to be affected;

(iii)   Appoint an experienced banker to advise the bank in the proper conduct of its affairs/business.

The guidelines further stated that the Central Bank of Nigeria should examine the position of each bank on a continuous basis with respect to the stipulated criteria. It added that banks, which fail to meet the prescribed criteria, should not be allowed to grant further credit until compliance is achieved.

It further said that existing banks will be encouraged to continue to build up their capital base to strengthen their operations. In order to continue to encourage self-regulation in the banking industry, it said it will continue to enhance ethical standards and transparency in banking operations. In this regard therefore, the Central Bank of Nigeria has set up a sub-committee in ethics under the aegis of the Bankers' committee to address complaints from the public and operators within the banking system.

The Governor of the Central Bank of Nigeria was quoted as saying: -

"the Committee will be very useful, especially for those banks having bottled up feelings against the CBN or against one another which can be openly discussed. It will also provide an excellent forum for members of the public who have genuine complaints but are unable or unwilling to resort to a judicial process, to lodge complaints with the subcommittee".

The CBN further said it would be very firm in enforcing compliance with the capital adequacy ratio; minimum liquidity and cash reserve ratios. Continuing, it said that any bank which fails to maintain minimum standards will be given a maximum period within which to take corrective action, failing which drastic action against the bank including the withdrawal of banking license may be taken.

ACTIVITIES OF PRIMARY MORTGAGE INSTITUTIONS AND COMMUNITY BANKS

The Monetary Trade and Foreign Exchange Policy Guidelines for 2001, while commenting on the activities of Primary Mortgage institutions and Community Banks, stated as follows: -

"Pursuant to the mandate given to the Central Bank of Nigeria on financial market development, by the provisions of the CBN Act, 1991; and the Banks and other Financial Institutions (BOFI) Act 1991, as amended, the supervisory and regulatory framework for

Mortgage Institutions and the Community Banks will be strengthened in fiscal 2001 to ensure their viability and soundness, as well as enhance their effectiveness".

On a final note, however, the Monetary Policy Guidelines stated that all institutions are required to comply fully with the provisions of the relevant legislation and guidelines. It warned that any financial institution that fails to comply with the existing and revised guidelines issued by the CBN, as well as other directives as CBN may issue from time to time; or fail to furnish within the stipulated time any statistical and other returns as the CBN may from time to time prescribe will be appropriately fined as determined by the CBN or penalized as provided for the enabling law.

CHAPTER THIRTEEN

BANKER AND CUSTOMER RELATIONSHIP

13.1   WHAT IS A BANKING INSTITUTION?

Throughout English law and Nigerian Ordinances, there has not been any statutory definition of who or what a banker is. However, a number of British Acts of Parliament have tried to give a partial definition of a banker, or a banking institution.

a. Section 2 of the U. K. Bills of Exchange Act 1882 states that: 'banker' includes a body of persons whether incorporated or not who carry on the business of banking.

b. 'Bank' means any firm, incorporated company or society, carrying on banking business and approved by the Minister – (U. K. Agricultural Credits Acts, 1928, S.5).

c. Another acceptable or recognized definition is given by Halsbury's Laws of England which stated in its definition that: -

"a banker must receive money on current or deposit account, collects the proceeds of cheques by customers on himself".

It should be noticed from the definition in (c) above that a banker performs three principal functions as follows: -

i.   He must receive money on current or deposit account;

ii.   Collects the proceeds of cheques for his customers, and

iii.   Pays cheques drawn by his customers on himself.

The above attributes of a genuine banker were recognized in the leading case of United Dominions Trust Limited V. Kirk-wood (1960).

In Nigeria, the first banking legislation came out in 1952, but prior to that time banking was almost a free-for-all affair. It did not receive any special recognition, but was treated just like any other business activity.

However, as a result of several bank failures and consequent loss of funds by depositors, the government felt there was need to regulate banks. This resulted in setting up the Paton Commission in 1948 whose report led to the promulgation of the Banking Ordinance of 1952. In the Paton Report, it defined banking as follows:

> "The business of receiving from the public on current account money, which is to be repayable on demand by cheque, and of making advances to customers."

The 1952 Ordinance restricted establishment of banks and its practice only to companies granted valid licenses by the Colonial government.

The definition above was modified by the Ordinances of 1958 and 1962; but the Banking Act of 1969 then defined banking business as follows:

> "The business of receiving monies from outside sources as deposits irrespective of the payment of interest, and the granting of money loans and acceptance of credits, or the purchase of bills and cheques, or the purchase and sales of securities for account of others, or the incurring of the obligation to acquire claims in respect of loans prior to their maturity or the assumption or guarantees and other warranties for others, or the effecting of transfers and clearings and such other transactions as the commissioner may, on the recommendation of the Central Bank, by order published in the Federal Gazette designated as banking business".

From the above definition therefore, it could be seen that in Nigeria any person doing the business of banking as defined above could be called a banker, and this includes commercial, merchant, mortgage, development banks, community and peoples' bank of Nigeria. It is thus clear that discount and acceptance houses, including finance companies are not to be regarded as banks.

13.1.1 REQUIREMENTS FOR ISSUING A BANKING LICENCE IN NIGERIA ARE AS FOLLOWS:

i. Incorporation of a limited liability company under the Companies Act of 1968, and a copy of the latest balance sheet of the company. ii. Submission of a feasibility study of the proposed bank including the names and CV (Curriculum Vitae) of the directors and shareholders.

iii. Application for a banking license should be channeled to the Central Bank of Nigeria who would first scrutinize the books of the company, after which it recommends to the Minister of Finance (where it is satisfied with the company's books).

iv. If the proposed bank intends to have foreign participation, the equity is shared in the ratio of 60:40, between Nigerians and foreigners. No Nigerian is allowed to own more than 5% of the equity within the 60% equity stipulated for indigenous participation.

v. The foreign associate (or correspondent bank) of the proposed banking institution must have an acceptable network of international branches and possess expertise in the particular field in which it intends to operate in Nigeria.

vi. The company must be prepared to submit an acceptable program of accelerated manpower training and deployment of Nigerians to top managerial positions within a short space of time.

vii.   A program of branch expansion particularly to the rural areas of the country must be submitted. However, this requirement is no longer necessary with the advent of Community Banking in Nigeria which has effectively taken over rural banking.

viii.   Capitalization of bank is presently as follows: -

- Commercial banks   ₦500 million

- Merchant banks   ₦500 million

The new capitalization to effect in 1996, but it was increased to ₦1 billion in 1999.

Once the Central Bank issues a banking license, the licensee bank is expected to maintain certain capital ratios. The Banking Act 1969, S.6(2) states that: "the minimum ratio which licensed banks shall maintain between their respective paid-up capital and all retained earnings on the one hand and their loans and advances on the other must be 12: 1". This regulation of 1969 still obtains in the industry presently. With regard to merchant banks, the Central Bank shall from time to time specify the ratio of the followings: -

i.   Deposits and call money held for other banks to be maintained in liquid assets;

ii.   Loans and advances to the bank's total assets; and

iii.   Total loans and advances that may be repayable within one year.

It should also be noted that any bank that fails to maintain any ratio specified above may not increase its loans and advances, and this could eventually lead to revocation of a banking license.

CHAPTER FOURTEEN

WHO IS A BANK'S CUSTOMER?

This question is difficult to answer because there is no statutory definition of who a bank's customer is. But going by the definition or the word 'customer', it connotes the relationship existing between one person(s) and another as a result of <u>continuous dealings.</u>

For instance, someone who makes regular purchases of his provisions from one shop or supermarket can be regarded as a customer of that shop, or business establishment. Applying this simple definition to the question above, it is important to note that for the relationship to exist there must be continuous dealing between both parties.

However, it is essential to remember that several people go to banks every day for one reason or another. Some people visit banks to cash their own cheques, or make withdrawals from savings accounts. Some go to cash cheques, bank drafts, or even make enquiries about one thing or another. There are even others who also go to banks to exchange their money or to buy stocks and shares, but generally they all see themselves as customers of banks as a result of the relationships described above. Despite all these, however it is very important for the banker to ascertain clearly who his customer is, especially for two main reasons: -

a. To be able to claim protection of section 2 of the Nigerian Bills of Exchange Act 1964, (or Section 4 of the UK Cheques Act of 1957) for their customer;

b. The usual contractual obligations which apply to someone from the moment he or she becomes established as a customer of the bank.

14.1   COMMENCEMENT OF BANKER/CUSTOMER RELATIONSHIP

Coming again to the question of who is a bank's customer, it is generally believed by banking educators and practitioners that the relationship arises when a person(s), firm, company, or society, etc. makes an offer to become a customer, which the bank duly accepts. It can thus be seen that the element of offer and acceptance (which is a cardinal issue in the law of contract) comes into play in the banker/customer relationship.

However, the bank may accept someone as a customer subject to the followings: -

a) A Condition Precedent: e.g., the bank may accept the applicant's offer on condition that he provides satisfactory references. In this case, the bank agrees to open the account for its prospective customer(s) on the understanding that he will produce satisfactory referees. But where the customer finds it impossible or is unable to get acceptable referees, then the banker would close his account and return the customer's deposit (if any) to him, though at the banker's own risk.

b) A Condition Subsequent: e.g., where there is agreement to open an account for the applicant immediately, but the right to close it is retained forthwith if satisfactory references are not ultimately received. It is generally believed that the relationship between a banker and his customer is essentially a contractual one, as mentioned earlier. Fundamentally, it is a relationship of debtor (the banker), and creditor (the customer).

But the roles are sometimes reversed especially when the banker is a lender of funds; he then becomes the creditor, whilst the customer becomes the debtor. The contractual nature of the relationship also implies that the rules of agent and principal exist between a banker and his customer.

However, the working relationship between both parties is therefore governed by the following rules:

i. The rules of agency, e.g. Where the banker acts as agent for his customer by collecting or paying cheques on behalf of its customer. ii. The general rules of contract, e.g. Where the banker is obliged by law to carry out certain other functions on behalf of its customer.

iii. The rules of bailor and bailee, for instance where the bankers collect certain items for safe keeping from its customers. iv. Several rules of banking practice evolved over the years, and having been recognized as binding between both parties.

It could thus be seen that the relationship only commences after the applicant has opened an account, (i.e., after proper or 'satisfactory references' have been received by the banker) and a cheque book issued, (in case of a current account).

Note that only the banker is in a position to determine what constitutes satisfactory reference. However, it is generally accepted in banking circles that customers who have operated current accounts for at least six months, could be allowed to introduce a new or prospective customer.

14.1.1 Who Can Really Be Regarded as Bank Customer?

A pertinent question often asked is this: -

Is it only current account holders that can be regarded as bank customers? What is the position of Deposit account holders, and Savings account customer? Are they also to be regarded as customers of the bank?

In order to effectively answer the above-stated questions, it is necessary to look at some decided cases on banker/customer relationships: -

a. <u>Great Western Railway Company Vs. London and County Banking Co. Ltd (1901)</u>

It was held that to make someone a customer of a bank there must be either a current or a deposit account, or some similar relationship. Thus, it was held that the continuous cashing of cheques over a long period for a person having no account in the bank does

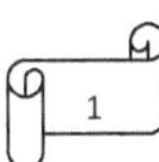

not make him a customer of the bank. There has to be an account of any sort to make someone a bank's customer.

The implication of this decision is two-fold:

(i) <u>On Savings and Deposit account holders:</u>

It could therefore be seen that both Deposit and Savings account holders can rightly be regarded as bank customers. The major difference between current account holders and those maintaining deposit and/or savings accounts is that the former produced satisfactory references before the accounts were opened; whereas deposit and/or savings account holders did not. However, some banks these days require deposit or saving account holders to produce referees if they wish to use such accounts for purposes of lodging cheques into their accounts.

(ii) <u>On depositors of items for safe keeping:</u>

There are sometimes, people who keep items of value with banks for safe keeping, but have not account whatsoever with the bank. In some cases, such a person is connected with someone who is in account with the bank (e.g. a house wife who deposits her gold trinkets with her husband's bank).

Perhaps no charge is made for such service, or in some cases a charge is made periodically which she settles in cash or by cheque drawn on another bank.

In this case, it would seem there is a banker/customer relationship also, and as such she may claim to be a customer of the bank. Though, under Nigerian situation she is expected to maintain at least a Savings Account, or be a joint account holder with the husband to be regarded as a customer.

b. <u>Lad broke & Co. vs Todd (1914)</u>

A thief opened an account with a cheque stolen from the plaintiff which he lodged with the banker Todd. The endorsement was forged, and he was not introduced to the bank, and no references were obtained. The cheque was specially cleared at the request of the thief who promptly withdrew the proceeds on the next day. The fraud was later discovered, but the drawers i.e. Ladbroke & Co) sent another cheque to the real payee, but sued the banker (Todd) in order to recover the proceeds of the previous cheques stolen by a thief.

The banker failed here because he made no inquiries about the cheque. He was therefore held to be negligent, but he was successful in claiming that he had collected the cheque for a customer. The judge also held that the banker would have been entitled to the protection of S.82 of the UK Bills of Exchange Act, (now S.4 of the Cheques Act 1957) which is similar to Section 2 of the Nigerian Bills of Exchange Act 1964 because he received payment for a customer. But the banker lost this protection because he was negligent by not making enquiries on the cheque before collecting it.

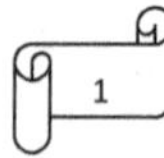

However, the judge ruled that the relationship of banker and customer begins as soon as an account is opened, and cash or cheques paid in for collection (not when money was paid out of the account).

c. <u>In Commissioner of Taxation vs English, Scottish and Australian Bank Ltd (1920)</u>

It was held by their lordships (i.e., the court judges), that a person whose money has been accepted by a bank on the understanding that it undertakes to honor cheques up to the balance in his account, is a customer of the bank. According to the judges, the word 'customer' signifies a relationship in which <u>duration is not of the essence.</u>

The ruling therefore signifies that once the banker has received money from a person on the understanding that it would honor cheques drawn on the account – up to its balance, then such a person is automatically a customer irrespective of whether his connection with the bank is of short or long duration; and whether or not satisfactory references were obtained by the banker before opening the account.

d. The formation of the Contract (banker/customer relationship) may be struck before the actual opening of the account, (e.g., in <u>Woods vs. Martins bank Ltd (1959))</u>. A person having no account consulted the bank manager for investment advice on certain money which was at that time lodged with a building society (or mortgage bank). Owing to the advice he received from the banker, he (banker) was authorized by this person to collect the money from the building society. He was also authorized to make some investment with most of it, and to retain the balance of the proceeds to be dealt with according to his (Woods) further instructions.

He opened a bank account three weeks after the date of giving his instructions to the banker transferring the money from the building society. It was held by the judge that the relationship of banker and customer started from the date the authority to collect the money was given to the banker. This ruling may be categorized under <u>condition precedent</u>, in which case the banker opens the account immediately; or where the status of customer exists, and is made on the condition that the reference given would become acceptable to the banker.

14.1.2 The Position of a 'Would-be Customer' or a Prospective Customer

It would be noticed that the judgments mentioned in the previous chapter do not take account of the status of a would-be customer, or a prospective account holder during the period references are being made on his suitability or otherwise to operate a current account.

In the early days, when banking was a much smaller and more or less personalized business than what it is now, a new customer was usually introduced by an existing customer. The existing customer normally brought the prospective customer to see the branch manager and introduced him personally, and completes/signs the banks' reference forms immediately. Up till today, many banks' account opening forms reflect these procedures with spaces for the name, address, occupation and specimen signature of the new customer together with a space for the referee's signature, name and account

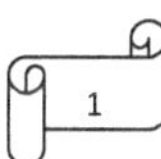

number. Where banks use this method of introduction, the whole process is done at once and there is no delay resulting in references being taken. In fact, the current account could be opened within one day.

CHAPTER FIFTEEN

BANK LENDING, MORTGAGES AND SECURITIES

Before lending to its customers, bankers usually attach much importance to character of the borrower. The following are the factors of credit worthiness which bankers consider before lending: - they are five and include Capital, Capacity, Collateral, Conditions and Character.

In Summary

Capital- Means the assets of the borrower or company.

Capacity- is the earning power, viability or profitability of the business concern or the borrowers.

Collateral- this stands for the asset that was pledged as security for a loan (or lending) request by the prospective borrower.

Conditions- this refers to the borrower's experience and capability in the activity, or business performance of the applicant for the banking facility.

Character- this refers to the integrity of the person wishing to borrow money from the bank.

According to Prof. Uzoaga, a former Lecturer of Banking in the University of Nigeria, Nsukka, he stated that: "Character of the borrower is a very important consideration for the banker in a loan or lending proposition." However, he further stressed that a man in possession of the excess of the first four factors but lacks character is not qualified for a loan, because one without character can have the money but refuses to repay the loan.

The question now is this: - how will the banker determine the character of a customer who wishes to borrow money from the bank? Customers must operate their bank accounts for at least six months period before applying for banking facilities, as this period would enable the bank to study the customer's character, through the intending borrowers' method of banking operations and other interactions with the banker.

Additionally, the Central Bank of Nigeria (CBN) recently introduced what it called KYC system also known as Know Your Customer initiatives. Through this method, banks are mandated by the CBN to ensure that they get to know properly who their customers truly are. Banks therefore hold frequent interactive meetings with their customers and which offers bankers a means of getting closer to them. Some banks then set up Customers' Relations offices through which they maintain closer relationships with customers, rather than the old system whereby bank customers were regarded as mere account numbers by most bankers.

Consequently, most banks now hold quarterly meetings with their customers, more intensive visits to customers especially the small, medium and self-employed operators to find ways of developing mutually beneficial relationships.

Finally, most banks also organize what is called "Customers Forum" and End-of-Year parties which gives room for fruitful interactions between the banks and their customers. At this forum, bank customers have opportunities to discuss or ventilate their feelings regarding the bank and its officers. It is however observed by Banking Professionals and others, that the KYC Scheme has really brought a lot of improvement in Bankers/Customers relationship because they now realize that the "Customer is King", and cannot be treated with levity, anymore.

Consequently, the banks have recently become an interesting place for pleasant and mutually beneficial business interaction, unlike what obtained in the past.

WHAT IS A MORTGAGE?

A mortgage refers to a legal agreement that conveys conditional right of ownership of a property (typically landed), by its owner to a lender as security for a loan (www.businessdictionary.com.). In Nigeria, where the majority of the citizenry are of the middle class socio-economic standing, purchasing a home fully funded by private capital might be a herculean task and will probably take many years of savings to accomplish.

A mortgage however reverses that system. How? Instead of saving for about 20 years to finally be able to afford a home, a mortgage can help you purchase the home, and then pay gradually over a period of that same 20 years.

The body set up by the Federal Government to cater to this Nigeria is the National Housing Funding (NHF). There are also several other commercial mortgage facilitators, and almost every bank has a mortgage arm from which clients can obtain a loan.

How Does the Process Work?

Mortgages are also loans which mean that they come with interest rates. Typical mortgage *interest rates in Nigeria range between 7-10% for the NHF and between 1525% for commercial mortgage institutions*. Aside from the interest payable, the potential buyer must also have a certain percentage of the total amount needed for the purchase readily available; *this amount is known as equity* and should range between 30-70% of the total cost of the home.

Another important factor to consider is *the tenor of the loan*; this is the length of time required to pay back the loan. *In most situations in Nigeria, the maximum amount of time given is 20 years*. When approaching any mortgage institution for a loan, the most important factor they will consider before approving your request is your income. *Ideally, mortgage payments should not take more than 25-30% of your monthly income*, this ensures that you still have enough to be able to take care of other responsibilities and hence, do not default on your loan payments.

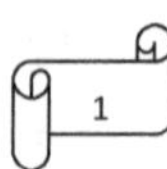

What Documents Do You Need?

Requirements may vary depending on the institution but the items listed below are always constant as follows: -

- A Comprehensive statement of account (12 months or more, as required by the lending bank.)
- Employment and confirmation letter (if employed)
- Certificate of Incorporation of business (if in business)
- Nationally accepted means of identification
- Utility bills
- Application form (provided by mortgage institution or lending bank.)
- Original title deed of property (To confirm that property is not in contest).

Please take note that similar documents as stated above are also required by banks whenever they are considering lending to borrowers seeking Bank Loans or Overdrafts from their banks. Consequently, all the above-stated process and documents pertaining to Mortgage Agreements for Mortgages or NHF also apply to bank customers who seek loan and overdraft.

In Nigeria, a lot of people are still very skeptical about taking home mortgages; however, this is one of the surest and easiest ways of owning your own home. I advise that you sit down and do a proper analysis of the financials to see if a mortgage can be in the works for you.

Also, if you're concerned of being overly burdened with paying off interests, I recommend trying out the National Housing Fund as their interest rates are significantly lower. However, this will only work if you're seeking a small loan as their maximum loan amount is ₦15million. On the upside, if you don't have a lot of equity, this will still work for you as the NHF can finance up to 90% of the cost of the cost of the home.

Home Ownership & Mortgages in Nigeria.

The number of people who own their Homes is one of the very major indices of measuring economic growth and the development of the people of any country; that is after food and clothing. In Nigeria, the ability of a majority of individuals to use their private resources to build their own homes have been hampered by dwindling purchasing power, high interest rates, high inflation, a weak national housing strategy, among others. Resort to alternative sources of funding like accessing Mortgage Loans or commercial loans, etc. have left many financially disadvantaged and emotionally scaled.

Mortgage transactions have been entered into by desiring home owners without sufficient information, or non-disclosure of all the obligations required by the Financial or Mortgage Institution or Co-operative Society from the intending home owner. Allegations of high interest rates- which are usually compounded-wrong and hidden charges and debits to the Mortgage Loan Accounts, non-availability of legal documentation securing the Mortgage transaction, short term and astronomical increase in costs of building materials, non-delivery of full or half-completed homes with weak structures, unilateral increase in the value of the Mortgage Loan, etc. remains rampant with no visible and timely protection for the desiring home owner, from either the Housing Regulators or the judicial system.

The Housing Regulators are handicapped to discharge their statutory duties by many factors which include insufficient legal, regulatory duties by many factors which include insufficient legal, regulatory and budgetary constraints.

This Alert is our further contribution to assist you in making an informed decision when contemplating or entering into a Mortgage arrangement in your quest to own your own Home. Where you are undertaking an outright purchase of a property, we have on our web site- www.oseroghoassociates.com- a September 2002 Alert/Checklist to assist you also in that process.

What is Mortgage?

A Mortgage is a form of security, on land or a complete building or buildings, given by a person for a loan advanced to that person to acquire land or a landed property. The Mortgage naturally gets terminated when the debt is repaid. ***The person taking the Loan is called Mortgagor while the Lender is called the Mortgagee.***

It is essential and much more preferred that you have a Mortgage Agreement that is in writing. This written document enumerates the terms and conditions of the Mortgage, including the repayment plan with interest rates to be charged on the loan, the powers of the Mortgage Lender to exercise his power of sale or appoint a Receiver to sell the property without resort to lengthy litigation, insurance, etc.

The absence of a written Mortgage Agreement means that only an equitable interest would be created when the Lender disburses to the Borrower the loan to purchase the property. This is in contrast to a Legal Mortgage.

An equitable interest could arise in the following situations: (a) By a mere deposit of title deeds by the borrower to the Lender. (b) By an agreement to execute a formal legal mortgage between the Borrower and the Lender. (c) By a mere equitable charge on the property. The above mentioned methods of creating an equitable Mortgage all have the unpleasant handicap of requiring the Mortgage Lender to go to Court to enforce his rights where there is a default in the repayment of the Mortgage Loan by the Mortgagor/Borrower.

The reliefs open to the Mortgagee with an equitable Mortgage, depending on the wording of the equitable Mortgage or the transactional documents available, include (a) an application to a Court of Law for specific performance of the agreement between the Borrower and Lender to execute a Legal Mortgage (b) A Court Order for foreclosure so that the lender can recover the amount lent from the sale or otherwise of the property.

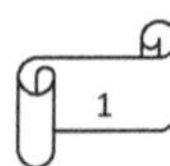

(c) An Order of Court authorizing the Lender to sell the property himself or appoint a Receiver/Auctioneer to sell the property to recover the amount owed.

Checklist for Negotiating a Mortgage or Bank Facility (Loan or Overdraft).

In considering whether to finance the purchase of your home yourself or resort to a Mortgage arrangement, you may need to consider the following: -

1.   Your housing budget and affordability vis-à-vis your other daily needs. Note that the standard housing budget for an income earner is an average of 30% of your current monthly income.

2.   The Location of your desired home and home prices in that location.

3.   Choosing a property and undertaking property visitation. Visit the property at least twice, on different days and times of the day. On at least one occasion, visit the property independent of any agent, and maybe with a spouse or a friend, for independent decision. Never negotiate these visitation or home prices, etc on the telephone or by email.

4.   How much you currently have to finance the home purchase?

5.   How much you require to borrow? If you need to borrow, how do you obtain the Loan? If through a Mortgage Institution, which to choose? Ensure you visit all the financial institutions and listen to the substance of their pitch as opposed to the esthetics. Do not be embarrassed to ask many questions on situations that are unclear. Obtain referrals from present clients where possible.

6.   Have you disclosed up-front the full terms and conditions of the Mortgage Loan? Have these terms and conditions been formalized in a written Agreement. Where not possible, for whatever reason, withdraw from the negotiation.

7.   Inquire about any one-off or other major installment costs in the Mortgage and compare with your affordability? What happens to all your contributions should you elect to exit from the Mortgage arrangement or choose another Mortgage Institution or financing option?

8.   Choose a Solicitor for all your due diligence before you execute any document or write any Cheque or effect any payment. Ensure that he investigates the title to your desired property that it is free from all registered encumbrances. If there is none, have him prepare one and insist that it is executed.

9.   Also choose a registered Estate Surveyor & Valuer to advice and provide independent information about properties, their locations, market prices and funding options including Mortgage Institutions. A fixed retainer as opposed to a commission agent is suggested to maintain the attention of the Estate Valuer.

10. Where there is a contractor in the mix, request for a copy of the construction contract as the outcome of that contract is your property. If not allowed, do not write a Cheque or execute the Mortgage Agreement.

Mortgagor's Covenants.

Some of the covenants that you as a Mortgagor should expect to find in a Mortgage Agreement includes: -

1. Punctual payment of both the principal amount and the interest on the Mortgage Loan with provisions for penalties for late repayments, etc.

2. Insurance on the Mortgaged property with the Mortgagor and the Mortgagee's interest disclosed on the Insurance Policy.

3. Repayment of the Mortgage Loan to be made during a defined and certain period. Exemptions to be indicated.

4. Right of the Mortgagee to consolidate the Mortgagor's Mortgages where there are more than one Mortgage Loan or property.

5. Power of sale by the Mortgagee and condition precedent to the exercise of that power or similar rights.

6. Mortgagor's right to lease or grant licenses subject to Mortgagee's consent.

Handicaps to Mortgage Business in Nigeria.

There are many reasons why many Nigerians are unable to own their own homes or access mortgage facilities to own one. In stating some of these reasons for your appreciation, you would be more vigilant when choosing a Mortgage firm or other financial Institution. Some of the handicaps include: -

1. Unavailability of long term funds for long term financing of housing projects.

2. High inflation.

3. An inefficient land tenure system which has been described as cumbersome, bureaucratic and one of the most expensive in the world when transferring title. There is also a lot of real estate whose titles are not registered.

4. Similar to 3 above is a cumbersome land registration, titling and conveyance procedures.

5. Low levels of participation by employers and employees in the National Housing Fund Scheme (NHFS), non-remittance of deductions by employers under NHFS,

reluctance of financial institutions to invest in the NHFS as a result of low interest rate returns from the Scheme, etc.

6. Deviation of the Mortgage Banks from their core Mortgage business to more profitable short term businesses like Commercial banks.

7. Insufficient legal and regulatory framework for Mortgage finance.

Conclusion

Ensure that you are always well informed and calm at all times when negotiating a property transaction. Undertake all due diligence that you can humanly have undertaken. In the short run, it is wiser to pay professionals a token fee than have your interest compromised in the long run. This is especially as the old adage recommends that "prevention is better that cure". Lastly, remember that once your money leaves your possession and control, it can become very expensive to get it back or have its value delivered, should things go terribly wrong.

SECURITIES FOR BANK LENDING

Definition of Security

The advanced Learners' Dictionary defines security as, "Something valuable such as landed property or life assurance policy, given as a pledge for the repayment of a loan or the fulfillment of a promise or undertaking". Security is also defined as "document, certificate, or something showing ownership of property (especially bonds, stocks and shares of government securities) for money lent to an individual or organization."

From the definitions above, it could thus be seen that securities are tangible instruments (such as Certificates) evidencing ownership of property, or stocks, shares and government bonds/securities. It also includes title deeds such as Certificate, etc., or other evidence of property ownership.

PURPOSE OF SECURITY

Bankers require security before lending to their customers in order to be assured of the safety of the advance, and also for the following reasons: -

(i)   It is a well-known fact that bankers can only lend part of the deposits or funds in their possession. As these funds are depositors' money, the banker has to ensure that customers would be capable of repaying the money (or ensuring its safety) by obtaining appropriate security from the borrower(s).

(ii)   Bankers have to ensure that money lent will be re-paid hence the necessity for accepting securities from borrowers (which will be disposed of) in case of default.

(iii)   It is also an acknowledged banking norm or practice that securities must be obtained from borrowers before any lending could be undertaken. The Central Bank of Nigeria regulations also stipulate that no bank should lend money without obtaining adequate and tangible security. This measure is to ensure banking prudence among bankers, and also guard against excess liquidity in the economy.

TYPES OF SECURITIES

There are various types of securities for lending but the following are the most common: Land or buildings, life assurance policies, stocks and shares, Debentures, Cash Deposits, Domiciliation of Payment, Guarantees, etc. others are: - Bills of exchange, promissory notes and documents of title to goods (evidenced by a trust letter or deed), etc.

LAND

Land or property

In Nigerian as well as English Law, the word 'property' refers to land and whatever is attached to it like buildings and economic trees standing on it. The definition of land in both the English and Nigerian Law is quite wide, but section 5.3 of the Interpretation Act Cap. 89 of the Laws of the Federation of Nigeria, 1985, give a definition of land. This statutory definition defines land as: "That immovable property which includes land and everything attached to the earth, or permanently fastened to anything which is attached to the earth and all chattels real".

Definition of land according to the statute above, also includes abstract incorporeal rights, like a right of many and other easements as well as profits enjoyed by one person over the ground, and building belonging to another. In English law there is a similar principle which states that whatever is affixed to the soil belong to it.

Land or landed property (which also includes building), are the commonest and most acceptable security for lending by bankers (and finance houses) in the country. The reason is because unlike other types of securities, land appreciates in value over the years and it is equally marketable and reliable as a security for bank lending. In contrast however, chattels and other movable assets do not possess this intrinsic quality which land possesses, hence its ready or easy acceptability by bankers as security. However, it has to be emphasized that for our purposes, property refers to land and buildings (especially developed land). This is because, banks and financial institutions in Nigeria accept only developed land (or properties) as security instead of undeveloped land. Land will also be used here to include both developed and undeveloped land, but there may be need to differentiate one from the other as the need arises.

TITLE TO LAND

Title to land in Nigeria can be evidenced by any of the followings despite the changes brought into our land system by the Land Use Act of 1978 which also recognized these titles to land.

The various titles are: -

   (a) Deeds of Freehold;
   (b) Deeds of Conveyances and Leaseholds;
   (c) Assignments of Freeholds or Leaseholds
   (d) Certificate of Occupancy (C of O)

It is however worthy to note that the land Use Act of 1978 apart from recognizing the above-mentioned titles to land, also converted all interests in land to either a statutory right of Occupancy, or Customary right of Occupancy for lands located in urban centers and rural areas respectively.

LAND USE ACT OF 1978

This Act brought a lot of radical changes to the Nigerian land ownership system, and it is of extreme importance to bankers and students alike.

As stated in the preamble to the above Act, the main objectives of the Land Use Act are: "to ensure, protect and preserve the rights of all Nigerians to use and enjoy land in Nigeria, and the natural fruits thereof in sufficient quantity, to enable them provide for the sustenance of themselves and their families". As a consequence of this, the Act thus vested in the Federal Government or its agencies (and the state Governors) all land (both State and federal). They are to hold the land in trust and administer it for the use and common benefit of all Nigerians. The Act further stipulates that what any person in Nigeria can mortgage or alienate is his <u>Right of Occupancy</u> and for which he/she requires the prior consent of the Governor of the State; otherwise, it is void and cannot be enforced by the courts.

<u>The following are the main provisions of the Land Use Act of 1978:</u>

   (i)   As from the 29th March 1978, no individual could have freehold interest in land, but however it recognized those already having such (and similar interests) before the enactment of the Act. Consequently, it became un-lawful for any person to prepare freehold conveyance or other similar titles to land as from that date.

   (ii)   The Act introduced the use of Certificate of Occupancy throughout Nigeria as the acceptable legal title to land, viz.

           (a) <u>Statutory Right of Occupancy</u>

It is granted by the Governor of a State for land located in urban centers of the state

(b) <u>Customary Right of Occupancy</u>

It is granted by the Chairman of a local Government Area for land located in the rural areas. Consent to Mortgage a customary right of occupancy to land is granted by the local government Chairman, whereas the consent to mortgage a statutory right of occupancy is granted by the governor of the State or any other functionary to whom it is delegated by the governor.

(iii) Section 50(I) of the Act defined developed land as land where there exists any physical improvement in the nature of road development services, water, electricity, drainage, building structure (including fencing), or such improvement that may enhance the value of the land for industrial, agricultural and residential purposes."

(iv) As a result of the Land Use Act, only developed land became recognized by bankers as security for lending. This is primarily as a result of the fact that the Act stipulates that in case of compulsory acquisition of land or revocation of right of occupancy by a State Governor, compensation for undeveloped land is limited to an amount equal to the rent (if any) paid by the occupier during the year in which such right was revoked.

(v) Though there are provisions under Section 29(4) of Land Use Act for payment of compensation where land has been compulsorily acquired, the maximum payable for one hectare of undeveloped land in Lagos metropolis is ₦7500.00 only. This amount is considered the highest compensation payable anywhere in Nigeria; and it is also partly for this reason that bankers do not accept undeveloped land as security. This is because the amount of compensation payable for un-developed land is too meager.

(vi) The Certificate of occupancy thus became the most important and acceptable title document to land in Nigeria. However, it is absolutely un-necessary to obtain the certificate in connection with leases, conveyances and assignment of land, which were executed, stamped and registered before the date the Act was promulgated. Consequently, the above-named documents are still regarded as valid title documents, and are accepted by bankers as securities for lending. But for the transaction to be valid, the appropriate consent to deal with the property must be obtained from the authorities as stated earlier.

(b) <u>Difference between a Charge and a Mortgage:</u>

A Mortgage as defined above, is the conveying (or conveyance) of an interest in land or property with the understanding that this right will be reconveyed to the borrower after repayment of the debt.

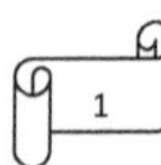

A charge on the other hand conveys some legal interest on the mortgaged property rather than a legal estate. The value of a charge by way of legal mortgage is that the banker (or charge) has the same (or similar rights) and remedies as if it was created under a term of years absolute. A charge conveys nothing but merely gives the charge certain rights over the property.

(c)   <u>Nature of legal Mortgage</u>

A   legal Mortgage is a security created by contract between the bank and the borrower, for the repayment of a debt already due (or to become due soon thereafter). It should be noted however that the debt is totally independent of the mortgage, which it exists to secure. Consequently, if a house which is mortgaged to secure a loan is destroyed by fire or flood, the debtor is still liable to repay the debt. Hence bankers always insist on borrowers taking up insurance policies to cover any property being offered as security.

(d)   <u>Nature of Equitable Mortgage</u>

An equitable mortgage is created where the mortgagor (or borrower) deposits the title deeds (or documents) of the land or property, accompanied by an informal document or memorandum of deposit under hand. A mortgage is also equitable where the mortgagor has only an equitable interest in the land, it means that the depositor (or borrower) has an equity of redemption after repaying the debt.

It is normal practice (under equitable mortgage) that the deposit of title documents should be accompanied by a Memorandum of Deposit. But a Memorandum of Deposit may not be necessary if it can otherwise be proved that the deposit was made with the intention of using the title documents as security for a debt. This intention is presumed in the case of a deposit of title documents with a banker, but it is for the depositor (or borrower) to prove the contrary.

However, to be on the safer side and to avoid controversy, it is advisable to obtain from the depositor some memorandum (or any document at all) signed by him however informal, which evidences that the deposit is intended as security for a debt.

It should be noted that a simple deposit of title deeds accompanied by a memorandum of deposit is not required to be stamped or registered since the interest of the mortgagee is created not by the memorandum, but by the deposit of title documents. An equitable mortgage evidenced by a memorandum of deposit, and an Irrevocable Power of Attorney requires stamping and registration. But ordinarily, an equitable mortgage does not necessarily require such elaborate formalities. Note that an equitable mortgagee has nearly the same rights as a legal mortgagee, but those rights cannot be exercised without the court's help.

DISADVANTAGES OF EQUITABLE MORTGAGES

(i)   In case of default, it cannot be enforced by sale except by order of a court. As a result of the consequent court proceedings, most bankers do not readily accept equitable mortgages.

(ii)   A subsequent purchaser or mortgagee of the legal title without notice of a prior equitable mortgage takes free of the equitable interest. In conclusion therefore, it is clear since the commencement of the Land Use Act 1978, that

> what is being mortgaged is in fact not the land, but the right of occupancy whether arising by operation of the Act or not. However, one must not lose sight of our definition of land, which includes improvements upon the land, and cannot be transferred or mortgaged in any meaningful sense without the land itself. And for bankers therefore, what is being mortgaged is the improvement or development on the land by way of buildings and rights to them, and not the land itself (which is vested in the Governor) by virtue of the Land Use Act 1978.

(iii)   It should also be noted that the general attitude of some bankers who would not accept any other document of title except certificates of occupancy is not correct. This is because the Land Use Act of 1978 also recognizes other previous title to land as discussed earlier in the chapter.

THE POWERS AND REMEDIES OF A LEGAL MORTGAGEE

It is normal practice to set out the powers and remedies of a legal mortgagee in the instrument of legal mortgage. They are as follows: -

(i) The right of foreclosure is a right which the banker (or Mortgagee) can exercise if the Mortgagor fails, after due notice to make repayment of the debt when due.

Where there is any discrepancy, the banker has to reject the document but if there is none then he has to proceed further. The photocopy of title document has to be handed over to the bank's solicitor who would conduct a search at the Land Registry.

The purpose of the search is to confirm that the borrower is in fact the owner of the property. Secondly, if the borrower is truly the owner the search will reveal whether the property was previously mortgaged or charged in favor of any other person; bank or finance house. It will also reveal if there were any encumbrances or encroachments on the land.

The production of the original title document of land showing the customer or borrower as the owner is not always a conclusive evidence that he is the true owner of the land, or the interest in question. The bank's solicitors must trace the customer's root of title as prescribed by law, after which a <u>Certificate of good title</u> is issued by the solicitor if satisfied as to the borrower's title. It is equally important for the banker to conduct a search at the company's Registry (now called Corporate Affairs Commission) if a company wishes to borrow. Banks also conduct a physical inspection of the property whereby a bank's staff visits the property to ensure that its location and structure are acceptable to the banker. A <u>certificate of physical inspection</u> is equally issued to certify the state of the property in question.

(i) <u>Valuation of the Property</u>

 Having been satisfied as to the borrower's title, the next step is to ascertain the value of the property being offered as security to the bank. It is the practice among bankers to ensure that the value of property offered as security far exceeds the amount of facility being requested by the borrower. This is very important in order to ensure that in the event of default, the amount realized from the sale of such property would cover the debt plus accrued interest.

The valuation could be undertaken by a senior and experienced bank official if the amount of facility being sought is not much. This is sometimes allowed by bankers in order to save the customer from the clutches of professional estate valuers whose charges are usually quite high.

Bankers do not normally accept valuation reports prepared by the customers' own valuers for fear that such reports could have been inflated in order to assign a higher value to the property than it is actually worth. The only exception is where the valuation report was prepared by one of the bankers' approved estate valuers (otherwise it would be rejected by the bank).

A valuation report is normally undertaken by firms of professional estate valuers. The report is a confidential information/report submitted by the estate valuer and designed to guide the banker by enabling him decide whether the security offered is appropriate or adequate. Property valuation is normally based on its' open market' value. This refers to the estimated price at which the property would easily or readily be disposed of in case the borrower defaults. The banker having ascertained the value of property being offered as security would ensure that its value far exceeds the amount of facility being sought by the borrower. As a rule, bankers do not lend more than a fair percentage of the value of property offered as security.

For instance, where a property is valued for say ₦100,000.00, the banker is not obliged to lend more than ₦60,000.00. This is often done in order to leave the banker with a safe margin, so that in case of default the bank might be able to realize a reasonable amount on disposal of the security.

(iii) <u>Obtaining the necessary consent</u>

Under the Land Act of 1978, the Mortgagee has to obtain the consent of the Governor of the State (or Chairman of the Local Government Council) in all dealings on land.

It is mandatory to obtain this consent before any assignment, letting, or parting with possession of State land under the Land Use Act of 1978. It should also be noted that a right of occupancy under the Act is not valid without the Consent of the State Governor or the Chairman of a local Government (for land Located under the local government).

Also, alienation (or parting with the property) is both illegal and void if the consent was not obtained. The consent is not super-imposed on the right of occupancy, but rather is an intrinsic component of it. It should also be noted that the acquisition of non-state land by an alien from a Nigeria citizen requires the consent and approval of the state Governor, otherwise such transfer will be rendered null and void. It has to be emphasized that the statute also provides that a covenant not to alienate (or transfer property) with the –Governor's consent shall be implied in every lease of state land. In practice however, all leases of state land contain an express covenant to that effect, but the effect of the provision in the statute is that even in the absence of an express stipulation in the lease, the covenant will nevertheless be implied; and the lease is to be deemed to contain it. The breach of this covenant is not a contravention of a statutory prohibition which attracts the sanction of illegality and voidness; it is a breach of contract and is redressable by the award of compensation or by forfeiture where that is provided for in the lease.

(iv)   <u>Execution of the legal mortgage</u>

Having obtained the necessary consent, the next step is the signing of the instrument of legal mortgage by both parties, (i.e., the Mortgagor and mortgagee).

The mortgagor is required to sign the legal mortgage in the presence of the banker manager, his Assistant or Branch Accountant, who will also sign as a witness. If the mortgagor is a limited liability company then its managing Director will sign with the company Secretary; after which they affix the company's seal to the document.

This document is then counter-signed by the banker's Managing Director (or any Director so delegated), and the banker's Secretary after which the banker's seal is affixed to the document.

If the customer is illiterate, special care has to be taken to comply with the provisions of the illiterate protection law regarding the execution of documents by illiterate persons. Failure to comply with the provisions regarding illiterate persons may result in the security document being un-enforceable, or altogether void. The banker has to ensure that the deed contains an <u>illiterate jurat</u>, and the execution of the document must be done in the presence of a Magistrate.

The jurat is a kind of certification by the Magistrate to the effect that the wordings of the legal document have been read and interpreted to the borrower who understood its contents. Thereafter, the borrower appends his/her mark, or right hand thumb impression on the document. It is also required that any person who completes this

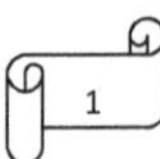

security document must write inside the document his/her own name as the writer thereof, his address and the fees charged (if any) in accordance with Illiterates Protection Ordinance (Cap 83).

CHAPTER SIXTEEN

FINANCIAL INTELLIGENCE FOR ALL AND WHY PEOPLE WRITE BOOKS

The theoretical framework for the Study of Financial Intelligence was set by organizational development experts/academics like Dennis Dennison, Edward Laura and Alfred Pheffaer of USA. It has since gained momentum in academia, as research and academic institutions have developed programs on the subject of financial intelligence.

There are four broad areas of understanding financial intelligence, namely: -

i.   Understanding the foundation;

ii.   Understanding the art and science of accounting,

iii. Understanding trend analysis, etc. and

iv.   Understanding what we call "the big picture."

These four principles of financial intelligence led to excellence, informed decision making and proper evaluation of facts and realities of any given situation.

Financial intelligence is important because it helps one to secure a place in today's business world and in life generally.

The Bible says: "money answereth all things". But we should read this along with the scripture that says: "the love of money is the root of all evil". Please, note that <u>we should not be motivated by the love of money,</u> but by the thought of the good we can use money to do in our society.

<u>Financial intelligence constitutes the knowledge,</u> the skills of understanding finance and accounting principles.

<u>It teaches you how money</u> is applied profitably and diligently.

<u>It inculcates the techniques and approaches</u> of expending assigned funds, such as:- salaries, allowances, profit from businesses (or corporate/company net profits), entrepreneur endeavors, or even gifts and inheritances.

<u>At the Corporate Level:-</u> Financial intelligence emerged as best practice and core competence principle for improved financial results, as well as increased employee's morale and reduced employee's turnover.

This lecture was delivered by Akwa Ibom State Governor, Mr. Udom Emmanuel, at the monthly "Holy Ghost Service" of the Redeemed Christian Church of God (RCCG) at the Redemption Camp, Lagos-Ibadan Expressway on 11th October 2020, under the theme – "The Bright and Morning Star". The Governor, a Chartered Accountant and former Banker promptly acknowledged that the choice of the theme, "the Bright and Morning Star" and "Financial Intelligence" as a sub-theme made him quite comfortable because he was on a comfortable turf.

In the lecture, he also outlined attitudes and traits that are common to the financially intelligent person (both youth and adult), no matter their status in life. The governor said that financially intelligent people:

- ❖ <u>Are Action oriented:</u> "they create what I call comprehensive and workable financial plans that they may implement and manage diligently".
- ❖ Have a saving mentality: they utilize their savings for investment purposes and compound their money for long-term gains. He said "for example, Joseph in the Bible was financially intelligent and through saving, he saved Egypt from famine".
- ❖ Shy away from liabilities: when they buy, they search for the best at lowest prices before making a final decision.
- ❖ Set short, medium and long-term goals. You cannot live a life purposefully without setting goals to motivate you.
- ❖ Regularly seek professional advice to multiply their wealth. How we mitigate our risk will determine who is more successful than the rest of us.
- ❖ Absorb, imbibe and adapt the characteristics, habits and rituals of those who had made successes of such practices.
- ❖ Never stop learning about money:
  When God wanted to give Solomon wisdom, He gave him wisdom and also gave him money.

On the "Foxes" that militate against financial intelligence, he said that "little foxes" are the situations that take away resources from our businesses, and incomes. He identified some of the foxes that reduce financial intelligence as:

Instant gratification, which is the fox that keeps people perpetually in debt. Financially intelligent people will defer gratification, and be led to spend a fraction of profits and invest the rest for the joy of tomorrow. He also said that they prefer to endure the "cross" today, because it is not safe to spend everything we earn.

The second "fox" is living in denial. Governor Udom Emmanuel explained that when we say, "I am not interested in money; or money is not everything," we are living in self denial. According to him, "the Bible says: 'Money answereth all things,' and we can't claim to know more than the Bible. Although we are warned not to worship money, we need money for our well-being and that of others. We even need money to spread the gospel.'

The third fox, according to him is, the blame game: i.e., blaming others and looking for excuses. He noted that blaming others and finding excuses is human nature, but you must be conscious of this, because blaming everyone for our inabilities and manufacturing excuses for our failures affect our financial intelligence. "You are the captain of your own ship," he stressed. "We have to find a way of getting rid of the foxes that steal our financial intelligence," he reiterated.

Using what you have; the God-loving Governor went back to biblical teaching, saying, "Remember that in Proverbs 22:1, the Bible says: A good name is rather to be chosen than great riches, and loving favor rather than silver and gold." He said, "Make money God's way; and reject making it Satan's way! Also, the problem in today's world is that many people have sight, but they don't have vision at all. Have a vision, run with it; it is for an appointed time, that is what the Bible says."

In Habakkuk 2:3, the Bible says: "For the vision is yet for the appointed time, but at the end it shall speak, and not lie; though it tarry, wait for it; because it will surely come, it will not tarry."

In conclusion he said, "you should know that all what you have is what you need to get to where the Almighty God has destined for you. Remember that all your treasures are within you."

Culled from Real Life Forum by Bisi Daniels, Sunday Sun issue, page 12, November 1st, 2020.

Why People Write Books

The answer to this question is provided by Mr. George Orwell, whose real name is Eric Arthur Blair, the 18th century English author of the then popular book, "Animal Farm" – alias "all animals are equal, but some are more equal than others".

It was a political satire which mirrored what was happening at that time in England. Mr. George Orwell said, "putting aside the need to earn a living," there are four great motives for writing a book: -

- ❖ The first reason is what he calls "sheer egoism," i.e., the desire to be talked about and to be remembered after death.

- ❖ The second is "aesthetic enthusiasm" – the desire to share an experience which one feels is valuable and ought not to be missed.

- ❖ The third reason is what he calls "historical impulse," i.e. – to discover facts and store them for posterity.

- ❖ The fourth reason why people write books, according to Orwell, is for "political purpose," ie – the desire to push the world in a certain direction through writing a book or books.

I strongly believe that the above-stated reasons are strong enough to motivate anybody wishing to write books of any type in the world, despite the present internet age.
However, it is very important to encourage our reading and writing culture in order to bring about economic and political development to our country.

SECTION C

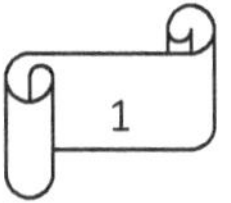

CHAPTER SEVENTEEN

DEFINITION AND INTERPRETATION OF MANAGEMENT

Introduction

Not unexpected, the variety of approaches to the theoretical background of management have produced their own persons of what is meant by such key words as "management" and "organization." This book looks at eh most typical variation in the interpretation of such words and offers some explanations.

The Meaning of Management

There is no generally accepted definition of "management" as an activity, although the classic definition in skill held to be that of Henri Fayol. His general statement about management skill remains valid after fifty years and has only been adapted by more recent writer, as shown below:

Henri Fayol (1916)

"To manage is to forecast and plan, to organize, to command, to co-ordinate and to control."

E.F.L Breach (1957)

Management is a social process:

The process consists of: planning, control, coordination and motivation.

Kootz and O'Donnell (1976)

Managing is an operational process initially best dissected by analyzing the managerial functions. "The five essential managerial functions (are): planning, organizing, staffing, directing and leading and controlling.

The changes made by Brech, Kootz and O'Donnell represent changes of emphasis rather than principle.

Simplification of submission above

It is to be recognized that the above definitions are extremely broad. Basically, what they are saying is that "management" is a process which enables organizations to achieve the objectives by planning, organizing and controlling their resources including gaining to the commitment of their employees (motivation).

What is Administration

At one time the words "administration" and "management" were more or less interchangeable. Fayol himself used the French word "administration" to mean "management" in his original treatise on the subject. Nowadays "administration" tends to be understood as the narrower task of developing and maintaining procedures. That is to

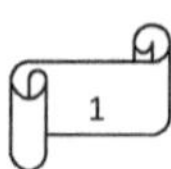

say, it is seen primarily as an aspect of organizing. This interpretation of administration is even becoming accepted in civil service, where at one time the word "management" did not form part of the official vocabulary.

FAYOL's Definition of Management

Fayol prefaces his famous definition of management (to forecast and plan etc.) by stating what he considers to be the key activities of any individual understanding. He outlines such activities;

- ❖ Technical activities e.g., production

- ❖ Commercial activities e.g., buying and selling

- ❖ Financial activities e.g., security capital

- ❖ Security activities e.g., safeguarding property

- ❖ Accounting activities e.g., providing financial information

- ❖ Managerial activities of planning and organizing

To manage, to command, to co-ordinate and to control. He sees forecasting and planning as looking to the future and drawing up a plan of action.

Organizing is seen in structural terms. Commanding is described as maintaining activity among the personnel. Co-ordinating is seen as essentially a unifying activity. Controlling means ensuring that things happen in accordance with established policies and practices. It is to note that Fayol does not see managerial activities as exclusively belonging to the management. Such activities of an undertaking. Having said thus, it is equally important to point out that Fayol's general principles of management take a perspective which essentially looks at organization from top downwards.

The General Principles of Management

In this book we will be looking at Fayol's fourteen "principles of management". These are the precepts, which he applied most frequently during his working life. He emphasizes that these principles are not absolutes but are capable of adaptation according to need.

He does not claim that his list is exhaustive, but only that it served him well in the past. The fourteen items listed are given in the order set out by Fayol.

The comments and a summary of his own are as follows:

Division of work:

Reduces the span of attention or effort for any one person or group. Develop practice and familiarity.

Authority:

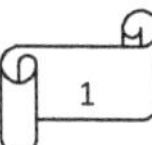

The right to give orders should not be considered without reference to responsibility.

Discipline:

Outward marks of respect in accordance with formal or informal agreements between firm and its employees. Unity of Command: One man, one superior

Unity of Direction:

One head and one plan for a group of activities with the same objectives.

Subordination of individual interests to the general interest:

The interest of one individual or one group should not prevail over the general good. This is a difficult area of management.

Remuneration:

Pay should be fair to both the employees and to the firm.

Centralization:

It is always present to a greater or lesser extent, depending on the size of company and quality of its managers.

Scalar Chain:

It is the line of authority from top to bottom of the organization.

Order;

A place for everything and everything in its place; the right man in the right place.

Equity:

A combination of kindliness and justice towards employees.

Stability of tenure of personnel:

Employees needs to be given time to settle into their jobs, even though this may take a lengthy period in the case of managers.

Initiative:

Within the limits of authority and discipline; and levels of staff should be encouraged to show initiative.

Esprit de corps:

Harmony is a great strength to an organization; teamwork should be encouraged.

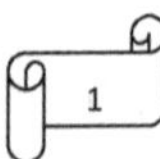

CHAPTER EIGHTEEN

THE SCIENTIFIC MANAGEMENT SCHOOL

The pioneers of Scientific Management include F. W. Taylor, Frank and Lillian Gilbreth and H. Gantt.

The last twenty years or so of the nineteenth century were a time of facing up to the often ugly realities of factory life. From the employers' point of view, efficiency of working methods was the dominant issue. The gathering pace of the industrial revolution in the Western World had given rise to new factories, new plant and machinery, labor was plentiful. The problem was how to organize all these elements into efficient and profitable operations.

It was against this background that Taylor developed his ideas. He was passionately interested in the efficiency of working methods. At an early stage he realized that the key to such problems lay in the systematic analysis of work. Experience, both as a worker and as a manager, had convinced him that few, if any, workers put more than the minimal effort into their daily work. He described this tendency as "Soldiering" which he subdivided into "natural" soldiering i.e., man's natural tendency to take things easy, and "systematic" soldiership i.e., the deliberate and organized restrictions of the work rate by the employees. The reason for soldiering appeared to Taylor to arise from three issues:

❖ Fear of employment

❖ Fluctuation in the earnings from piece-rate systems

❖ Rule of thumb methods permitted by Management

Taylor's answers to these issues were to practice "Scientific Management".

<u>The Principles of Scientific Management.</u>

Taylor recognized that what he was proposing would appear to be more than just a new method – it would be revolutionary. He stated at the outset that scientific management would require a complete mental revolution on the part of both management and workers.

In its application to management, the scientific approach required the following steps:

❖ Develop a science for each operation to replace opinion and rule of thumb.

❖ Determine accurately from the science the correct time and method for each job.

❖ Set up a suitable organization to take all responsibility from the worker except that of actual job performance.

❖ Select and train workers.

1

❖ Accept that management itself be governed by the science developed for each operation and surrender its arbitrary power over the workers i.e., co-operate with them.

Taylor saw that if changes were to take place at the shop floor level, the facts would have to be substituted for opinion and guess work. This would be done by studying the jobs of a sample of especially skilled workers, noting each operation and timing it with a stopwatch.

All unnecessary movement could then be eliminated in order to produce the best method of doing a job. This best method would become the standard to be used for all like jobs. This analytical approach has come to be known as work-study.

BENEFITS OF THE SCIENTIFIC MANAGEMENT

The benefits arising from Scientific Management can be summarized as follows:

i. Its rational approach to the organization of work enabled tasks and processes to be measured with a considerable degree of accuracy.

ii. Measurement of tasks and processes provided useful information on which to base improvements in working methods, plant design, etc.

iii. By improving working methods, it brought enormous increases in productivity.

iv. It enabled employees to be paid by results and to take advantages of incentives payments.

v. It stimulated managements into adopting a more positive role in leadership at the shop-floor level.

vi. It contributed to major improvements in physical working conditions for employees.

vii. It provided the foundations on which modern work study and other quantitative techniques could be soundly based.

Limitations to Scientific Management

The drawbacks to scientific management were principally the following:

i. It reduced the worker's role to that of rigid adherence to methods and procedures over which he had no discretion.

ii. It led to the fragmentation of work on account of its emphasis on the analysis and organization of individual tasks or operations.

iii. It generated a "carrot and stick approach" to the motivation of employees by enabling pay to be geared tightly to output.

iv. It put the planning and control of workplace activities exclusively in the hands of the management.

v. It ruled out any realistic bargaining about wage rates since every job was measured, timed and rated "scientifically."

More issues on Scientific Management Theory

Whilst it is true that business and public organizations world over have benefited from, and are continuing to utilize techniques which have their origins in the scientific management movement, it is also a fact that in the west at any rate, a reaction against the basic philosophy of the creed is taking place. Tasks and processes are being reintegrated, the individual is demanding participation in the key decision-making processes, and management prerogatives are under challenge everywhere by individual and organized groups.

The most important outcome of scientific management was that it stimulated ideas and techniques for improving the systematic analysis of work at the workplace. It also undoubtedly provided a firm launch – pad for a wide variety of productivity improvements in a great range of industries and public services.

Its major disadvantages were that it subordinated the worker to the work system, and divorced the "doing" aspect of work from the planning and controlling aspects. There drawbacks led to:

The creation of boring repetitive jobs,

The introduction of system for tight control over work, and

The alienation of shop-floor employees from their management.

CHAPTER NINETEEN

BAD MANAGEMENT IN ENTERPRISES

Bad management is a situation where there is a breach or violation in the laid down managerial pattern or codes. It is a state whereby the expectation from the "manager" is overturned. For example, it is bad management when the organization plans to change functions in the coming month and the manager instead of doing just that decided to use the money to change all the cars in the organization; that is bad management.

Symptoms of Bad Management

1. Low productivity

2. Low/sales turnover

3. Incessant lateness to work by subordinate(s)

4. Overflows of retrenchment

5. Continuous retirement by personnel

6. Crisis among the staff

7. Hyper increment in administrative cost

8. Employment of unqualified personnel

REMEDIES

1. Policy overhauling of the management

2. Check and balances in the management crew

3. Disciplinary actions should be adopted for erring managers

4. Training and continuous training for the management

5. Experts should be employed as managers

6. Adoption of effective feedback system in the organization

CHAPTER TWENTY

BASIC PERSONNEL MANAGEMENT AND OFFICE ORGANIZATION

This section examines the human element in business management. It is recognized that the human factor is the most important in making things happen. Successful management depends on the attitudes of the manager and the managed. The entire work force must fully identify with the purpose and objectives of the business.

PERSONNEL MANAGEMENT

Personnel management involves managing people with their emotions, their instincts, their moods, aspirations and problems. The art of making people happy and keeping them is not easy. Those who achieve this are great personnel mangers as they may ensure higher levels of output than all the automation a company can assemble. This is because no matter how sophisticated, no tool can start and stop itself or make those essential decisions that ensure smooth operations. Operations which require judgment cannot be rushed or performed routinely and so far, only human beings are endowed with the necessary judgment.

The duty of the owner of the business or the personnel manager is to harness the human resources of his company in such a way that the objectives of the company are achieved with the greatest economy in time, resources and money. To achieve this aim, the owner of the business or the personnel officer must understand human nature, human behavior and use such understanding to advantage in setting personnel policies and carrying out his work. The personnel officer plays two roles in the company namely: -

a. The personnel officer has the role of guiding the board of directors in the determination of policy objectives and interpreting such policies; and assisting his colleagues, i.e., the production manager, the marketing manager, the controller- in executing the parts of the policies that directly concern them;

b. He or she has the role of running the personnel department which is charged with the responsibilities of ensuring that the right employees are found for the company, that they are adequately remunerated, promoted, trained and kept happy and motivated. Part of the latter duty is to maintain records of all employees; see to their health and social welfare and help to create the best possible working environment in the company.

BASIC PRINCIPLES OF PERSONNEL MANAGEMENT

Personnel management is an inseparable part the overall management system concerned with good industrial relations. It must achieve its goals through contact with and

1

consultations with all departments. Yet it carries specialized duties of a routine nature which tends to distinguish it as a special area.

The information of personnel policy is a central function which is the responsibility of the board of directors. Personnel specialists guide and assist such formulation and eventually execute those policies in collaboration with all other top officials.

Personnel policy

The general aim of personnel policy is to enable an organization carry out the essential desirable relations and objectives, resulting from the recognition of the fact that human beings have a free will to choose when to act and when to obey and when to disobey: to keep the employees fully informed and solicit their cooperation. The policy helps to create such conditions of employment as will make all employees develop a sincere sense of belonging, so that they carry out their duties willingly and effectively. It also constantly ensures that the organization has competent, able and willing employees for all levels of occupations. In addition to these, other specific objectives may be decided upon from time to time as the need arises.

OFFICE ORGANIZATION

The office plays a vital role in the smooth running of any business enterprise. It complements ad co-ordinates all the activities of various departments. The proper management of an office is therefore essential for the success of the business enterprise. Proper office management entails having well located spacious office buildings which are functionally adequate for their purpose. It further involves equipping the office with all necessary work aids, furniture and fixtures. Then the office must have a clearly set out line of authority and responsibility.

Information about the enterprise is gathered and kept in the office. The details of inflows (revenues) and outflows (expenditures) must be placed on record and carefully filed for easy references by the executive officers. Where cash sales occur and cashiers handle some cash, it is important to provide security through installing safes which are fire resistant and difficult to break.

The importance of an office can be brought out when it is realized that the office is used for the following purposes: -

1. For planning all production and sales.
2. For preparing and executing the budget.
3. For coordinating the activities leading to the acquisition of raw materials.
4. For calculating and payment of wages.
5. For keeping and analyzing all records.
6. For executive meetings where all decisions are made.
7. For production control purposes.
8. For financial budgeting, control and handling of cash.

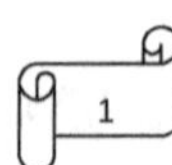

9. For receiving important visitors. It must be a pleasant place as many people will spend much of their life in the office.

There must be enough space for people to move freely around. The choice of an office system depends on what kind of business is involved. Very often, bankers work in an open office where all activities can be seen. This has the advantage that if any problems occur at any end, someone at another distant end can phone to security or sound an alarm. Workers have to get used to working in an open office since there tends to be a lot of distraction. The persons who have to concentrate are caged and made to face a wall, or the objects making the distractions less pronounced.

The open office has its disadvantages as it may lead to a quick spread of common cold. But its strength lies in the fact that idle workers are easily noticed. In some large offices where it is not possible to put all workers in the same open room, the manager may use a close circuit television to observe the activities of his workers in different rooms. Intercoms may also be installed to pass instructions or raise questions when unbecoming behavior is observed.

The closed office system with opaque partitions or solid walls provides privacy and allows concentration. Most higher executives require these closed offices for confidential work. They sometimes receive visitors and discuss very sensitive business and must avoid embarrassing their visitor. The closed office provides an air of dignity for top executives and even in banks, the top management stay in closed offices. But it must be noted that where partitions are permanently fixed, it is not so easy to rearrange the office and the number of workers accommodated is generally limited. In an open office with or without temporary partitioning, it is possible to rearrange the desks and equipment so as to add one or two. Smaller desks may be used to replace larger ones as the business expands and number of employees increases. The type of office arrangement solely depends on the type of business and what the owner of the business is comfortable with.

Organizational Charts

It is important to draw up a chart which shows every worker, the person to whom he is responsible. Each person should be answerable to only one superior (and perhaps through him to a higher officer). In this way confusion will be avoided and personality conflicts averted. The span of authority should be set according to complexity of the operation and the capacity of the worker. People should be used in their most effective positions. The fewer the managers, the easier the two-way communications in the establishment.

An essential fact of the organization chart is that it shows individuals where they are on the ladder and what to aspire to become, certain technical men have a limit to which they can rise, but any of the top managers can be promoted or appointed a director to take care of this special area at the policy making level. A business set up without a clear organizational chart does not inspire any worker. At times when people rise to the top of their chart, they become frustrated after several years when there is nothing to aspire to any longer. The management then has to be very imaginative and create challenges for them while continuing to ensure good incentives. For some companies which have branches, a hardworking man in such a position may be sent to go and revamp another branch.

MARKETING MANAGEMENT

Marketing is a vital function of any business concern which entails the formulation of policy guidelines and methods of ensuring the sale and distribution of a company's product. No one can continue in business if their products do not continue to find buyers willing to pay the prices that cover both the production and marketing costs, and also leave a margin of profit. The market which represents the amount of money a particular product that can be sold at a given time, determines the levels of production. All other company plans are based on an estimation of the market potentials.

The scope of Marketing Management covers: -

(a)   The determination of essential policies for marking;

(b)   Market research which determines the size of market for the business and shows the company's share of it, also indicates how to maintain or increase the share of market.

(c)   Sales promotion is meant to ensure that the products continue to be sold and encourages occasional upsurges in sales volume.

(d)   Sales forecasting and budgeting are very important tools in this regard.

(e)   Advertising management is meant to create effective demand and keep the products constantly in the minds of the consumers.

(f)   Sales records and statistics, their analysis and use for future planning are also important tools here.

(g)   The creation and maintenance of an effective sales force is very essential in Marketing Management.

The Consumers desire must be constantly reviewed and met. The best marketing manager is ahead by anticipating consumer tastes and preferences and providing these. This is where marketing research comes in; a product may be abandoned, modified or given other new look before the consumers show waning interest in it.

Purchasing

An important part of marketing management is the purchasing of either raw materials or goods to be resold. This has to be properly managed in order to place the company on a good footing right from the onset. To manage purchasing properly requires up-to-date knowledge of the particular industry. The qualities and prices of various goods and

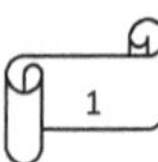

anticipated innovations in the industry must be well known. The purchasing department must not be caught buying the obsolete, out of fashion goods. Long standing contracts may be used to remove serious fluctuations in prices and obtain generous discounts.

Sales Management

On the sales angle, nothing can promote sales better than a consistent image of good, dependable quality. The company may require initial push, but once established, the goods sell themselves if quality is maintained. A mistake often made is that some businesses start well, create a good image which brings everyone to their door steps, but as soon as they are doing well, they reduce the quality and hence destroy the basis of their good performance. You cannot deceive all the people, all the time.

Sales promotion is expected to increase the volume of sales thus ensuring better use of installed capacity and minimizing unit costs. But the efforts must be sustained to avoid slipping back and fluctuations which hurt the business. Workers may have to be laid off temporarily, weekly purchases may drop, and then, the concession or discounts.

Conclusion

To manage the sales effectively, attention must be given to what the competitors are doing, the prices, given the qualities of product. What substitute exist and how useful, how big the market is and what is the company's share of it, whether new products are needed or the old should be increased; or whether small modifications in the old will be kept, sell more units such as in new models of the same basic car. Is the sales force adequate? Are the sales facilities like showroom, warehouse, transport, display facilities adequate? Are the sales men and managers satisfied and motivated. What other assistance do such people need in their areas? How should advertising be carried out? Regular or intermittent huge program, prime time on television or special columns in Newspapers; feature articles etc.? Any need for use of demonstration or after sales service? Training of salesman. Development of new sales channels and better methods of distribution. Reviewing the sales organization to keep it trim, yet affective so on so forth. these and others are important issues to be considered by to management for improved sales by the company or organization to survive.

CHAPTER TWENTY ONE

ORGANIZATIONAL STRUCTURE'S INTRODUCTION

1.	The study of the structuring of work organization is a developing field, it was of major interest to classical theorists such as Fayol, Urwick and Breach. It was the sources of inspiration for Weber's theory of bureaucracy and it is now a major feature of the theorists of complex organization- the contingency school. This chapter looks at the practical issues of structure facing modern organizations, and identifies the most important options that are currently available.

2.	As Lawrence and Lorsch have pointed out, most organizations are in a state of tension as a result of the need to be both differentiated and integrated. Once an organization has grown beyond the point when the owner can exercise direct control, then some degree of differentiation, of specialization, is inevitable. Thus, most organizations have to face up to a number of crucial issues, about the kind of structure that will best sustain the success of the enterprise. The most frequent issues are:

    a.	To what extent should we encourage the specialization of roles?

    b.	What degree of standardization should be imposed on behavior and methods, or to put it another way, what degree of discretion should be allowed to individual job-holders?

    c.	How much formality should be encouraged?

    d.	How many levels of authority should we establish?

    e.	To what extent should decision-making be centralized or de-centralized?

There is no perfect answer to any of these questions, but there are a number of possible, issues which, taken together can produce an optimum design for an organization. These will be considered shortly. First of all, we shall look more closely at the key issues, commencing with the question of specialization.

SPECIALIZATION

3.	Specialization is concerned with the division of labor within an organization. It serves to break down the total mission of an organization into a number of subordinate objectives which in turn give rise to tasks of various kinds. It is essentially a disintegrating process. This process acts initially by grouping key activities in the organization, and subsequently by allocating roles and tasks to individuals.

4.	Specialization by grouping of activities can be achieved in several different ways. The most frequent method is that of *functional specialization*. In this case, tasks are linked together on the basis of common functions. So all production activities or all

1

financial activities are grouped into a single function which undertakes all these tasks required of that function. A typical organization chart of a functional organization would appear as follows:

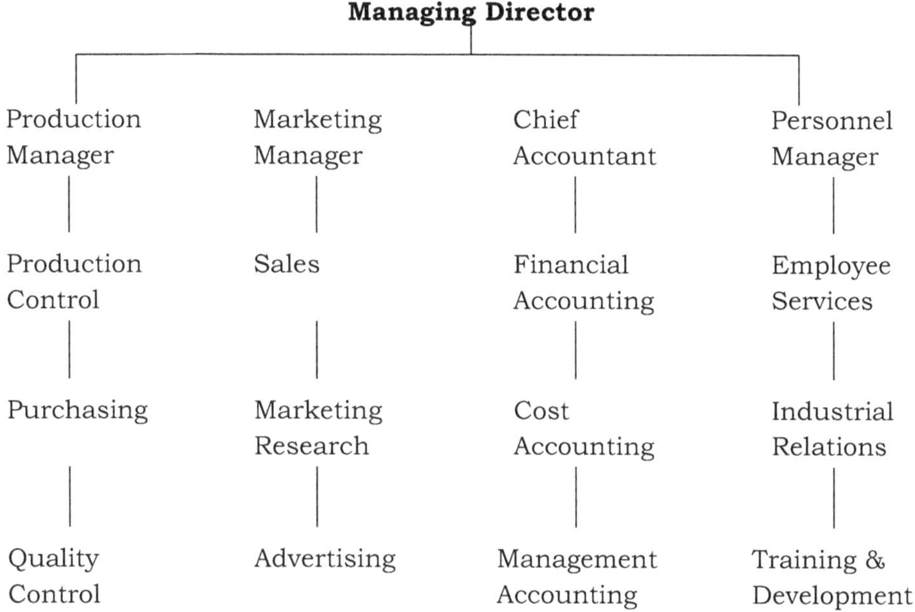

Figure 19.1 Functional Organization Structure

The main advantages of functional organization are that by grouping people together on the basis of their technical and specialist expertise, the organization can facilitate both their utilization and coordination in the services of the whole enterprise. Functional grouping also provides better opportunities for promotion and career development. The disadvantages are primarily the growth of sectional interests which may conflict with the needs of the organization as a whole, and the difficulties of adapting this form of organization to meet issues such as product diversification or geographical dispersant.

5. Another frequent form of grouping is by product. This is popular with large organizations having a wide range of products or services. In the National Health Service, for example, the key groups of employees-medical, nursing, para-medical and hotel services-are dispersed according to the service provided viz, maternity, orthopedic, surgical, psychiatric and many others. By comparison, a large pharmaceutical company could be organized as follows:

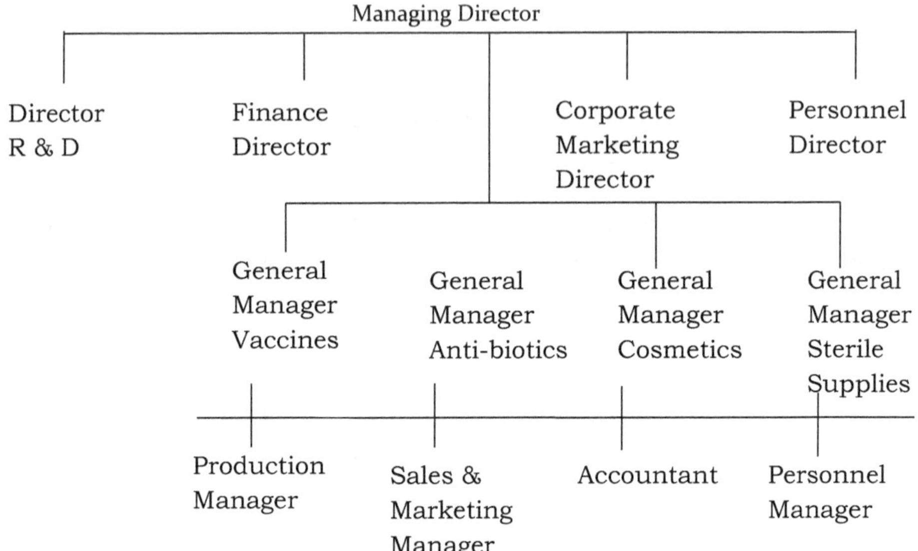

Figure19.2. Example of a product- based structure

The advantages of a product organization as shown are that it enables diversification to take place, it can cope better with problems of technological change by grouping people with expertise and their specialized equipment in one major unit.

The main disadvantage is that each General Manager may promote his own product group in a way that creates problems with other parts of the company. This implies that top management must exercise careful controls, without at the same time robbing the product managers of their motivation to produce results.

6. Another popular form of organization is grouped on a geographical basis. This is usually adopted where the realities of a national or international network of activities make some kind of regional structure essential for decision-making and control, in particular, an example of this form of organization is as follows: -

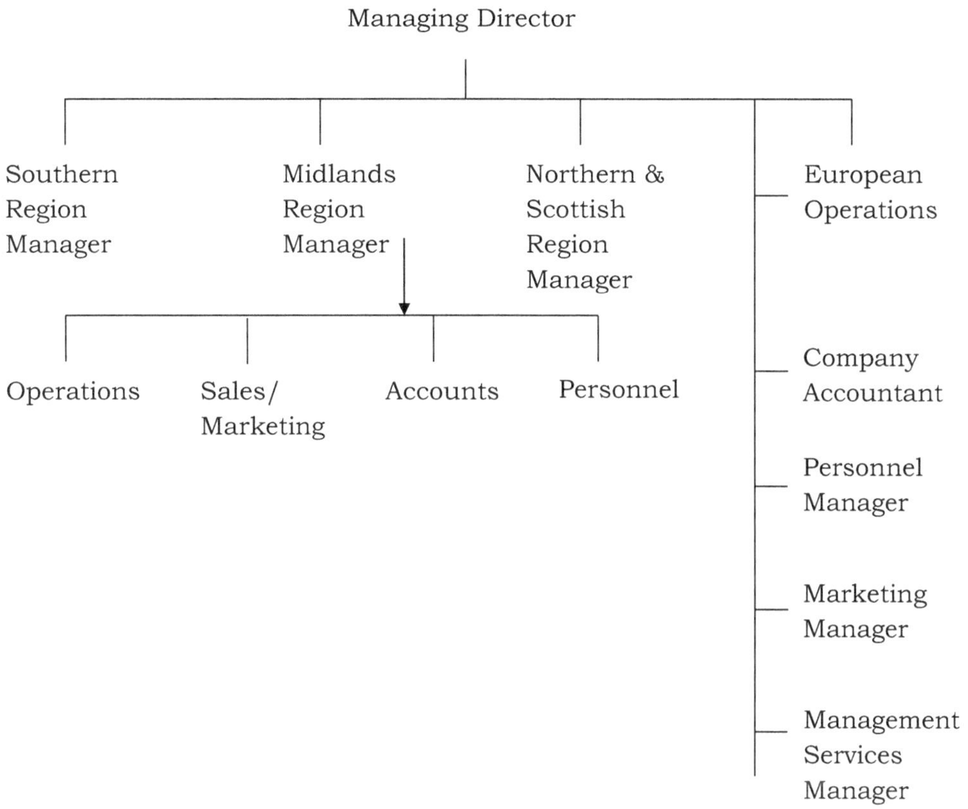

Managing Director

Southern Region Manager | Midlands Region Manager | Northern & Scottish Region Manager | European Operations

Operations | Sales/ Marketing | Accounts | Personnel

European Operations

Company Accountant

Personnel Manager

Marketing Manager

Management Services Manager

Figure 19.3 Possible structure for a road transport company

As in product organization, the de-centralized structure produced, causes additional problems of top-management control. Hence it is usual to find a group of senior functional managers located at headquarters in order to provide direction and guidance for the regional managers in the performance of their line role.

7. With increasing complexity ad size, many companies are opting for a mixed structure, which may combine the benefits of two or more of functional, product

and geographical forms or organization. Two such mixed structures will be looked at briefly: divisionalized structures and matrix structures.

Divisionalized structure: In these cases, the organization is divided up into divisions on the basis of products and/or geography, and each division is operated in a functional

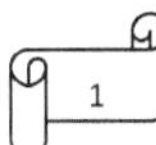

form, but certain key functions retained at company headquarters (e.g., planning, finance and personnel policy). This is becoming a common organization structure for highly diversified firms operating in more than one country.

ABOUT THE AUTHOR

Dr. Charles Obiora Ukemenam, is a retired Banker, Financial and Management Consultant. He holds both Masters and Doctoral Degrees from the University of Benin, Edo State Nigeria. He is also a Fellow of the Chartered Institute of Bankers (FCIB), London and Nigeria respectively; Member, the Institute of Management Consultants of Nigeria, IMCON, etc.

After serving in executive positions in some top Nigerian banks for a total period of twenty-five years, he retired voluntarily, and went into Business Education and Management Consultancy services.

He is currently the Managing Consultant/ CEO of ITCN Consults (Nigeria), Enugu. He was as well a Course Facilitator (or Lecturer), Department of Business and Human Resources Management, National Open University of Nigeria (NOUN), Enugu Study Centre for a period of five years. During that period, he handled Post Graduate programs, such as PGD (Post-graduate Diplomas), MBA, M.Sc., MPA, etc., and also supervision of final degree projects in the Department above-stated.

He was equally a former Senior Lecturer in Banking and Finance at two Polytechnics, namely: - IMT Enugu and Federal Polytechnic Oko, Anambra State for a period of six years in both institutions.

He is the author of **Practice of Banking for Students and Professionals**, published in 2001, and other books in motivation, self-development and entrepreneurial studies currently under publication.

ABOUT THE BOOK

Success and Motivation in Banking, Finance and Management, is a book which is greatly in demand especially in present day 21st century when millions of school leavers cannot find ready-made "white - collar jobs", anymore. Every year, universities and other higher institutions turn out thousands of graduates who cannot gain employment in offices because vacancies no longer exist to absorb new graduates, hence the urgent need to think outside the box.

The purpose of this book therefore is to teach unemployed graduates, retrenched/ retired workers, and others the importance of financial literacy for people wishing to embrace self- employment (or entrepreneurship), because white- collar jobs no longer exist. The book is properly designed and structured to fill this yawning gap in our country- and the world today.

Robert Kiyosaki, a renowned American investor and Management Consultant wrote that: "illiteracy, both in words and numbers, is the foundation of financial struggle. Something is misunderstood; the rich are rich because they are more literate in different areas than people who struggle financially.

In conclusion, he said.... "So, if you want to be rich and maintain your wealth, it is important to be financially, literate in words, as well as numbers". I agree totally and wholly with Mr. Kiyosaki, the renowned investor cum Management Consultant.

Author

BIBLIOGRAPHY/REFERENCES

Anderson, U.S (1971), <u>The Greatest Power In The Universe, California</u>, Wiltshire Book Company.

Anderson, U.S. (1968), <u>The Secret of Secrets</u>, California, Wiltshire Publishing Company.

Bland, Glenn (1983), <u>Success: The Glenn Bland Method</u>, Tyndale House Publishers, Inc. Wheaton, Illinois, USA.

Edwards J, and Melleth H, (2002), *Accountancy for Banking/Finance Students*, Chartered Institute of Bankers Londons, UK.

Ekwueme, Chi, (2020), *Management Theories, Principles and Techniques,* ASET Publishers (Nig) Limited, Enugu.

Ikpe L. E (1999), *Projecct Analysis and Evaluation*, Impression, Publishers, Lagos.

Ikpe L.E (1999), *A guide to Small Business Investments*, Impression Publishers Lagos.

Kiyosaki R (2000), *Rich Dad's Guide to Investing*, Warner Books, USA.

Kiyosaki R, and S. Lechter (2000). <u>Rich Dad, Poor Dad</u>, Warner Books Publication, USA.

Napoleon, Hill (1978), <u>Think and Grow Rich</u>, USA, Fawcett Publications Inc. Greenwich, Connecticut.

Napoleon Hill and E. Harold Keown (1971), <u>Succeed and Grow Rich Through Persuasion</u>, Fawcett Publications, Inc, Greenwich, Conn. USA.

Schuller Robert H.C. (1983), <u>Tough Times Never Last, But Tough People Do</u>. Thomas Nelson Inc., Nashville Tennesse, USA.

Paul J. Meyer, (2003), <u>Attitude is Everything</u>, Paul J. Meyer Resources, Waco, Texas USA.

Poisant C.A. and Godwin C. (2006). <u>Success Stories of Ten Millionaires</u>, Glasgow, Omnia Books Ltd.

Ukemenam, C.O. (2001), *Practice of Banking for Students and Professionals*, Enugu Oktek Publishers (Nig) Limited.

Ukemenam, C.O. (2011), <u>Financial Literacy and Entrepreneurship Development; Tools for Wealth Creation</u>. Oktek Publishers Nig. Ltd, Enugu, Nigeria.

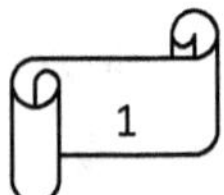

www.ingramcontent.com/pod-product-compliance
Lightning Source LLC
Chambersburg PA
CBHW061538120726
48001CB00004B/1622